Georgie Dent is a journalist, an editor, and a passionate advocate for gender equality. The former lawyer is a regular media commentator, public speaker and MC, and is the contributing editor of *Women's Agenda*.

Breaking Badly

First published in Australia in 2019 by Affirm Press,
a Simon & Schuster (Australia) Pty Limited company
Bunurong/Boon Wurrung Country
28 Thistlethwaite Street, South Melbourne VIC 3205

Affirm Press is located on the unceded land of the Bunurong/Boon Wurrung peoples of the Kulin Nation. Affirm Press pays respect to their Elders past and present.

New York Amsterdam/Antwerp London Toronto Sydney/Melbourne New Delhi
Visit our website at www.simonandschuster.com.au

AFFIRM PRESS and design are trademarks of Affirm Press Pty Ltd, Inc.,
used under licence by Simon & Schuster, LLC.

10 9 8 7 6 5 4 3 2 1

© Georgie Dent 2019

All rights reserved. No part of this publication may be reproduced, stored in a retrieval system, or transmitted in any form or by any means, electronic, mechanical, photocopying, recording or otherwise, without prior permission of the publisher.

The moral rights of the author have been asserted.

 A catalogue record for this book is available from the National Library of Australia

9781925712780 (paperback)
9781925870916 (ebook)

Cover design by Design by Committee
Typeset by J&M Typesetting
Printed and bound in Australia by Lightning Source

Breaking Badly

a memoir

Georgie Dent

For Mum and Nick.
For everything. Whether I was breaking, broken or better.

Introduction

'I've never seen any life transformation that didn't begin with the person in question finally getting tired of their own bullshit.'
Elizabeth Gilbert

This book seemed far more worthwhile before I signed a contract to produce it. Until then I had thought of it as a potentially useful read for anyone on the verge of breaking down or burning out, but in that moment it transformed into something totally indulgent: another story that the world did not need to hear. Rather than share the news of my publishing contract with anyone, I kept it secret for several weeks, almost embarrassed that this long-held dream was set to be realised.

Who, exactly, do you think you are to write a book? Why would anyone want to read what you *have to write? You are an online journalist, not an author, so I'm not sure who you think you're kidding.*

'The publisher has obviously made a huge mistake,' were the actual words I used when I finally told a friend it was happening. 'Either that or she feels sorry for me, so it's a sympathy offer.'

There was no false modesty in these disclosures; they were the only logical conclusions I could reach. My mind was an ants' nest, crawling with reasons I wasn't fit to author this book, why it didn't need writing, why it was self-absorbed of me to even consider writing it. Eventually a connection became so obvious that I could no longer ignore it: the doom through which I had been wading since signing the contract was precisely what precipitated this book in the first place.

At age 24, my life was almost a cliché. Six years of study were behind me, I was holding down a plum job as a lawyer in the city, I was living with my lovely boyfriend, I had great friends and the world was seemingly at my feet. From the outside it might have looked charmed; in truth it was anything but. I was miserable and chronically ill, my self-esteem was in tatters and I was strung out, constantly panicked and painfully thin. For twelve months I had been ignoring the worsening symptoms of my autoimmune disease, the heightened state of stress in which I existed, the self-loathing I couldn't overcome. I woke up day, after day, after day, ignored how wrecked I felt and kept pretending. I figured if I pushed aside my misery for long enough it would go away. It didn't.

It came to a head one night when I fell over at work with what I believed was a spell of vertigo, which developed into debilitating dizziness. It soon became apparent that it wasn't going to pass as quickly as it had arrived. Instead, it gathered momentum, and within a few weeks my life had crumbled around me.

I was unable to work, I moved back in with my parents and I spent four months either in bed or in various hospitals, unable to function. Physically I felt horrendous – my days were plagued with nausea, dizziness, weakness – and as my head continued to spin, my grip on the world slipped with every passing day. It culminated in depression and anxiety severe enough to warrant my admission to a psychiatric hospital for two weeks. One day, it seemed, I was an ordinarily functioning member of society, and the next I had been more or less sectioned, barely able to participate in the outside world.

How did that happen? What went so wrong? These are questions I was forced to examine forensically in the psychiatric hospital, and subjects I returned to regularly in the weeks, months and years afterwards. My nervous breakdown quickly became a landmark in my life that I couldn't – and didn't want to – forget.

The phrase 'nervous breakdown' is not used in medicine anymore, and it has no agreed-upon medical definition. It's an umbrella term that describes a period of intense mental distress where physical and emotional stress becomes intolerable, impairing the sufferer's ability to function effectively. This description matched my experience sufficiently well – perilously well, in truth – for me to say, unequivocally, that I suffered a breakdown.

It didn't happen because I had a traumatic childhood, suffered abuse or endured anything truly ghastly. With the exception of Crohn's disease, which can't aptly be described as a stroke of luck, my hand in life was more notable for its abundance of good fortune. I didn't fall apart because I had a nasty auto-immune condition or because I worked around the clock in a big law firm or because I was a natural-born worrier. I didn't fall apart because I developed anxiety. I fell apart and suffered a breakdown because I did not cut myself a break. Ever. About anything. Not about my health, not about my work, and certainly not about my mind. The consequences of this toxic habit cumulated over time and were eventually devastating: I unravelled physically, mentally and emotionally because of it.

Knowing that I was lucky and privileged only proved to be corrosive. I believed that because I had been lucky in many of life's lotteries, I had no justification for struggling or suffering.

As I began to write, this familiar, toxic habit was hard to resist. It was easy to tell myself that I wasn't qualified to write a book. That I had only suffered a breakdown because I couldn't hack the choices I'd made. That I was a terrible writer and that my breakdown didn't count because I hadn't ever suffered anything that could be considered traumatic. That it couldn't have been difficult because I had a family to help me through. Because I recovered.

You are probably just imagining that you had a breakdown so you can write this book. Has a more self-indulgent exercise ever been considered than this? Than YOU writing about your life as if you have a story worth telling? You weren't even good at English in high school. How could you possibly be qualified to write a memoir?

I felt almost nauseated with shame each time I sat down and sought to wrap words around the events that led to my breakdown. And then one afternoon, as I sat at my desk, staring at my blank screen, unable to type a single word because of this crippling doubt, something quite magical happened: I realised exactly why I might just be qualified to write this book. I lowered the metaphorical knife that I had been holding to my own throat, and in its place, I offered kindness.

You are scared, and that is perfectly reasonable. Writing a book isn't something you have done before. You have been offered a contract to write a book by a publisher because you are a writer and because you have a story to tell. You can do this.

It was a simple but seismic shift, and I remembered, not for the first time, how transformative my breakdown was. If you are looking for a Cliff's Notes version of my story it is this: I changed my life because I changed the way I thought. It was as complicated and straightforward as that.

Escaping the clutches of anxiety, which had escalated from moderate as a teenager to major as a young adult, was unbelievably liberating. I came to recognise the relentless expectations I had wielded over myself and, for the first time in my life, I wrested myself free from them. The difference was life-changing.

A decade on, I work as a journalist, an editor and a speaker. I am married to the man who was kind enough to ignore my frequent instructions, in the midst of my meltdown, to abandon this ship in search of a more stable vessel. We have three delightful daughters and, chaos notwithstanding, I am a (mostly) healthy, functioning adult. My 25-year old self wouldn't recognise me, and the sad and humbling truth of it is that she couldn't live the life I do. Not because my life after the age of twenty-five became vastly easier, but because I am not sure that she could sideline the fear and doubt that stopped her from doing what she wanted. The only reason I am able to do that now is that I broke so badly that the only way was up. If rock bottom has anything going for it, it has to be the clarity of perspective and purpose that crystallises in the dark.

Since I started speaking openly about my own breakdown, I have been struck by how many people have experienced something similar, or have watched a loved one go through it. My hope is that by being totally honest about falling apart, others will know they are not alone if – and when – it happens to them.

I can still vividly recall each day of the turmoil I experienced ten years ago. I remember how desperately alone I felt, despite the fact I wasn't actually alone. I had the love and support of family and friends, and the almost constant presence of someone to care for me. But I still believed that I was falling apart in a way no one else could understand.

Now, of course, I know that many, many people, young and old, for different reasons, will find themselves trapped in a place they don't like and can't escape. Not everyone will land themselves in a psychiatric hospital because of it, but life will test all of us. We will all have the wind knocked out of our sails at some point, and for many of us the aftermath of that won't be fleeting. But we don't always know what to do. We have rituals for celebrating many of life's happy milestones – weddings, births, anniversaries, graduations – yet when it comes to traversing the inevitable troughs of life, the monumentally difficult times, there is very little. We are ill-equipped to cope as individuals, but also as families, as workplaces, as friends, as a community; we don't know what to say or do when people break.

The good news is that even when you break in a calamitous fashion, when you seriously doubt you will ever feel happy or healthy again, it is possible to recover. There probably isn't a single pill, mantra, diet, yoga guru or acupuncturist who can magically resolve your turmoil (trust me, I tried everyone and everything), and the darkness won't disappear overnight, but it need not last forever. If you, or someone you love, is finding life increasingly difficult, I hope my story can help you plot your way out, even if it's merely by offering hope.

If you read this and find it indulgent, irritating and maddening to read, I need you to know, *I know*. I feel the same. Reliving it and writing it has been a torturous exercise, but unpicking the stories I told myself was unavoidable because that is what helped me pave a way out. And trust me when I say that however maddening it is to read, it was worse to live.

The best I can hope is that my experience might resonate with you, the reader, before you break. That you might recognise the pattern in your own mind and realise you can change it, and your life in the process.

Part One

Breaking

Faulty goods

November 2001

'I suspect you have endometriosis,' said the middle-aged gynaecologist, matter-of-factly.

Up until that moment I had never heard the word 'endometriosis', but apparently I was riddled with it.

'This wouldn't explain all of your symptoms, but it would explain the pelvic pain, so I will perform a laparoscopy to confirm the diagnosis and then, if I'm right, remove the tissue during another two procedures,' he continued.

The office was on the sixth floor of an old building on Wickham Terrace, a Brisbane street known for its congregation of medical specialists, and it was staid and stale. The beige carpet was faded, the upholstery on my chair was worn and the imposing desk between us was an anaemic-looking wood. There were beige frames on the walls displaying various certificates, but no drawings or family photos. Even the doctor looked beige.

'Endometriosis is a condition where cells similar to those that line the uterus creep around and attach themselves to other parts of your body, and it is one possible explanation for the symptoms you are experiencing,' the doctor explained.

This part of the appointment – sitting fully-dressed, engaged in an almost theoretical discussion about a condition that affects one in ten women – felt safe. I even felt a tinge of relief as it dawned on me that my troubled abdomen, the reason I was there, might be healed. But as we relocated to a small alcove barely a metre to the left of the doctor's desk for an internal ultrasound, I began to feel less certain.

'You can see here, that thickening,' he said, waving his finger across the screen beside me, pointing out areas of my anatomy that were blotted with darker matter that, to his eye, warranted a surgical investigation. To my eye he might as well have been pointing out an ultrasound image of a small dog: I could no sooner identify a thickening on my fallopian tube than I could identify my fallopian tube. The picture was a blur that, frankly, I wasn't enthusiastic to know more about.

The fact this medical exploration was wholly consensual and not remotely untoward did nothing to dim my discomfort. Positioned on a bed, pantless, with my legs in stirrups and a torturous-looking contraption investigating my inner workings, I wasn't in the best state of mind to absorb a tutorial on wayward endometrial tissue. At nineteen I was not yet accustomed to intimate medical procedures, and in this suffocating, sterile room I felt violated and vulnerable. The remnants of my early relief faded, along with my dignity, as the doctor outlined the procedures required to remove the trespassing cells.

'Endometriosis manifests itself most often in severe abdominal pain and can only be confirmed by a laparoscopy, where we take a selection of the tissue to biopsy,' he said. 'I will perform three surgical procedures over the next five weeks to have this tissue identified and then removed. The first and third procedures will be day surgeries and you will stay for a night or two for the middle operation.'

Okay, these are minor procedures, I told myself. *Two of them are only day surgeries. It isn't serious. There is no need to be dramatic!*

My attempt to stay calm was futile because, warranted or not, I was scared: the fight-or-flight instinct had set in and I'd opted to fly. Far away and fast. But I sensed this was not the reaction the specialist expected, going by his matter-of-fact manner.

Despite my best efforts I couldn't replicate my doctor's apathy, so I just pretended to. I spent the rest of the consultation feigning detachment while a lump the size of an orange formed in the back of my throat, and I blinked back what felt like a tsunami of tears. I nodded along as the plan for excising my endometrial tissue was mapped out and the doctor accompanied me on the short walk from the stuffy confines of his office to the communal desk where the receptionist was sitting.

As I fumbled for my wallet, took out my diary and pencilled in the various procedures, I avoided making eye-contact with anyone, terrified that they might notice my inner turmoil.

It wasn't until I stepped out into the sticky heat of Brisbane on the cusp of summer that I finally succumbed. I stumbled into my Toyota Corolla, pulled the door closed and sobbed.

Your body is like a derelict amusement park: nothing works. You're young but somehow there's always something wrong with you.

I was scared not only about the operations, but also about the broader implications of the diagnosis. I was in no hurry to have children, but to me this seemed a glaring indicator that my fertility might be compromised, and I was shaken.

I cried until my eyes were empty. When there were no tears left, I wiped my eyes and my nose and drove home.

~

If I had to pinpoint a single day that marked the beginning of my slow descent towards total breakdown, it would be that day: the 15th of November 2001. In that moment, it dawned on me that my body was truly flawed. I'd known for a while that something was awry. For at least the past two years my days had started, like clockwork, with a sharp twisting sensation in my abdomen that thrust me out of bed before I had properly woken up. I would rush to the bathroom in a semi-conscious state just in time for my stomach to purge itself. Beads of sweat would form on my brow, my heart would thump, and through a cloud of adrenaline, relief and pain, my days would begin.

This pain – and purging – came and went throughout the day, and despite the discomfort, it had become second-nature to ignore it. After a while, I grew so accustomed to this routine that I couldn't remember my days starting any other way. When I did think about it, I was mortified. At nineteen, living in Brisbane and working through a double degree in business and law, the intricacies of my digestive tract weren't exactly preferred topics to explore with my friends. So I kept it quiet.

This silence became much harder to maintain when my abdomen began regularly blowing up like a balloon. It would swell to resemble a half-term pregnant stomach, then it would become as tight as a drum before I began to feel stabbing cramps, like a pair of knitting needles were fighting ferociously in my belly. The pain was breathtaking, and it caused me to keel over on enough occasions to prompt a visit to a general practitioner, who referred me to the gynaecologist, an appointment that set me on the path to breakdown.

Obviously one medical diagnosis wasn't enough to single-handedly undermine my self-worth – that had been fractured to begin with – but it provided me with the first piece of tangible, physiological proof of something I had long suspected: I was faulty goods. The idea that I was broken, deficient and malfunctioning wriggled its way into my mind. Like the endometriosis wreaking havoc in my pelvis, these specks of shame settled in to tear at my self-esteem.

I was a natural-born worrier. For as long as I could remember, I had been permanently preoccupied with worries – big, small, highly likely and entirely fanciful. For me, worrying was the rule rather than the exception, and if I ever caught myself without an active worry, I immediately began worrying about whatever it was I had temporarily forgotten to worry about.

As a child I worried that my parents would separate, that my dad would die, that my mum would have an affair and that robbers would break in and kidnap my sister and me while we were sleeping. I worried that my aunt and uncle housed criminals because he was a lawyer, and in my small mind that meant he was in close contact with felons. (I was too young to know that a Glen Innes solicitor whose workload consists largely of property and estate matters barely has any contact with law-breaking citizens.)

I worried that my little brother would get sick, that a car accident would kill my whole family and that Dad would lose his job, even though he had his own business, so effectively worked for himself. I worried that snakes or spiders or dogs were lurking, ready to attack at the first opportunity. I was convinced that all white vans were driven by violent fiends who would lure children from schools with lollies before taking off with them.

These were not special-occasion concerns: these fears, and

many more manifestations, formed the silent soundtrack to my life. I cannot recall a time when my mind wasn't quietly consumed with the vague sense that disaster was imminent. Every film I watched fed my young mind a host of new concerns: I would physically recoil at the idea of a character being hurt, getting lost, being lied to, or suffering any fate that wasn't wholly comfortable and secure. Since comfortable, secure stories hardly lend themselves to dramatic interpretation, movie-watching was always fraught.

The first medical manifestation of my propensity towards worrying arose when I was just thirteen. I hadn't been at boarding school a year when a painful rash wrapped itself around my abdomen, which I showed the school nurse after a day of discomfort. She suspected shingles, an infection caused by the same virus that causes chickenpox, and promptly delivered me to the medical centre around the corner, where her diagnosis was confirmed. The GP who treated me said that it was highly peculiar for children to contract shingles, and that stress was almost certainly a factor.

Stress was most certainly a factor. It was 1996, and a few months earlier I had left my childhood home in Lismore for boarding school in Brisbane. Despite the obvious connotations, this was not because I was unloved, terrifically misbehaved or the offspring of ridiculously wealthy, cold parents who had no time to physically rear their sprog. It was merely the accepted rite of passage in our family. Both my parents had grown up in country New South Wales – my mum, Jan, in Grafton, and my dad, Michael, in Coonamble, a small town in the south-western plains – and they had both attended boarding schools in Sydney. They met as university students working at the Opera House bar in 1978, when Dad was in his final years studying dentistry and Mum was halfway through a speech pathology degree. After a brief courtship, they married and moved to Lismore, a town in the Northern Rivers where neither of them knew a soul, because there was an opening in a dental practice.

In October of 1980 they became first-time parents to my sister Belinda before I arrived in June of 1982. The arrival of my brother Chris in October of 1986 completed our family of five. Even though we weren't exactly country kids, the plan was always for each of us to board from Grade Nine onwards. It's impossible to avoid seeming elitist when you talk about attending a private boarding school, but it really wasn't framed that way. Mum and Dad were keen to give us the opportunities they'd had, and were eager for us to be familiar with city life, hoping it would make the eventual transition to university easier. We knew our parents were willing to make sacrifices to send us to boarding schools, but it was also made clear that if we weren't interested, we didn't have to go.

In Belinda's final year of primary school, the whole family drove up to Brisbane to have a look at high schools. My sister and I were both immediately taken with one breathtaking school on the fringe of the city. The boarding house was in a beautiful historical building, and we were transfixed by its every detail: the grounds, the facilities, the sea of girls we spotted making their way to an assembly, the different doonas that brought character to each of the dormitory beds. We left thrilled at the prospect of attending this grand institution.

Two years later, Belinda moved up to Brisbane to begin Grade Nine. I looked forward to each of her weekend and holiday visits, when she would fill me in on all the wondrous details of her exciting new life. I wanted to know all about her friends, her teachers, the rules, how prep worked, whether she could use that amazing gym we had explored and what was served for breakfast, lunch and dinner. My mind exploded with excitement at the picture she painted of boarding school. She didn't seem to suffer a single day of homesickness, and I assumed I would be the same.

I wasn't. From the very first moment I was delivered to this place I had dreamed of, I was desperately homesick. I had imagined unpacking my things into my very own cubicle would be a joyous activity, shared with the dorm-mates I'd assumed I would instantly befriend. I reality, I had never felt as lonely as I did standing in my cubicle alone for the first time. Not even the bright turquoise doona cover that I had been so thrilled to pick, and that Mum and Dad had helped fit to my bed just half an hour earlier, could alleviate the sinking feeling. This was nothing like I had imagined. I went straight to Belinda's cubicle, in a dorm across the hallway, and collapsed into her arms. There was half an hour before dinner and I spent every minute of it crying.

What was I thinking? Why did I think I would like starting at a new school? Why was it so fun for Belinda? Why doesn't she feel this awful? How am I ever going to stop crying?

When the bell rang to alert the hundred or so boarders that it was time for dinner, I tried to pull myself together. Belinda, and a few of her lively friends who had kindly tried to cajole me from my misery, walked me downstairs and delivered me to the table that would be mine for the whole term.

I was lonely and scared and felt like I had made the biggest mistake of my life. The little experiences that I had assumed would be tremendous fun – sharing a dinner table with twelve other people, watching TV in the common room, converging on the dining room for supper – were actually tremendously difficult.

Watching TV in a room jam-packed with pre-existing friendships isn't fun when you aren't part of any. The same goes for dinner, supper and every aspect of boarding-school life.

The next day, my first experience in the classroom, was worse again. Children start school at different times in Queensland and New South Wales, so even though I'd only finished Grade Seven at a local high school, my peers were all in Grade Nine. Since it had been determined that to fit in socially I should join the cohort of girls my own age, I had to skip Grade Eight entirely. Unsurprisingly, I was well behind the others in every subject.

I was out of my depth in every way: everyone else had had two years to get to know each other, *and* I couldn't keep up in class. (This goes some way to explaining why my Grade Nine bookshelf was dotted with titles such as *The Little Book of Calm* and *Don't Sweat the Small Stuff (And It's All Small Stuff)*.) For a girl with a tendency to stress, it was a recipe for disaster – or shingles, as it transpired.

It would take two whole terms for my homesickness to be displaced for good, when I finally got a hold on the school work and formed some actual friendships. The arrival of a new boarder in our grade named Harry, the most sophisticated fourteen-year-old I had ever seen, helped. We fell into an easy friendship, along with Cass, another boarder. Finally, I had friends, and the whole boarding school caper became properly fun.

Nevertheless, stress remained an ever-present problem for me throughout high school. I was known by both friends and teachers as a stress-head and was acutely aware that I worried a lot, but I simply couldn't comprehend that there might be another way to live. When friends and members of my family encouraged me to stress less, as they often did, I had no concept of how I might achieve that. They may as well have said to me, 'let's cure cancer'.

As I progressed through school, the frequency and intensity of my mental disquiet grew, but I assumed this heightened state of stress was inevitable. As someone who had been stressing about school since I started kindergarten, what were the chances of me gaining some perspective when the stakes were finally raised to the biggest bar of all, my leaving marks? Nil. It was during this final year of school that my stomach first began acting erratically on a regular basis. After I told Mum about it, she arranged for me to see a GP, who referred me to a gastroenterologist. He put it down to stress and assured me that it wasn't uncommon to see final year students with this problem. It would resolve itself once the year was done, he said. Of course, it didn't.

Curiously, mental illness is not a concept I remember having any awareness of at that point in my life. I knew that stress and worry were my mind's natural state, but had never considered that it might constitute a mental health condition. It's almost unfathomable now, given the breadth of the public conversation about mental health, but this was 2001. The information age, spurred by the ubiquity of the internet and greased by the proliferation of social media, online news and smartphones, wasn't yet upon us. Reading the newspaper was a ritual I enjoyed, but did mental illness crop up? Not that I can recall.

With the wisdom of hindsight and the context of evidence that suggests three in four adult mental health conditions emerge by age twenty-four, and half by age fourteen, it is more than likely I suffered from generalised anxiety well before I was diagnosed with it. And despite having no academic qualifications to make this diagnosis, I am confident this emerged before I turned fourteen.

A generalised anxiety disorder manifests itself in excessive worry about a variety of things, such as work or school performance. Someone experiencing generalised anxiety disorder may feel that their worries are out of control, feel tense and nervous most of the time, have trouble sleeping or find it hard to concentrate. That description pretty much sums up the first quarter of my life.

A battle and a boxing ring

January 2002

'Diet?' the balding specialist practically spat at my dad, peering impatiently over the rimless spectacles perched on the tip of his nose. 'Diet has *absolutely nothing* to do with the treatment of this disease.'

Another doctor's office; another uncomfortable conversation. It was late January, and Dad and I were in a small private hospital in Brisbane, learning about the latest addition to my list of physical ailments: Crohn's disease. The gastroenterologist's office was far shinier than the gynaecologist's, with monochrome art on the walls, a glass desk and modern furnishings, but his bedside manner was no more impressive. He had the air of an authoritarian school principal who would not have disputed the return of the cane.

'Medication treats Crohn's,' the doctor said, eyeballing Dad. 'She can eat and drink whatever she likes.'

You'd think Dad had just suggested that tea leaves were an adequate treatment for cancer rather than asking about the impact of diet on a digestive disease.

The endometriosis surgeries had been draining and seemingly ineffective, so the search for an answer had continued. The week before this appointment I had undergone the indignity of my very first colonoscopy, which had unfortunately confirmed that an auto-immune condition was the culprit behind my stomach's erratic purging. Crohn's, which is every bit as vile as it sounds, causes inflammation in the digestive tract, which can cause abdominal pain, severe diarrhoea, fatigue and malnutrition.

'It is managed more often than it is cured,' the charmless medic informed me. 'It is not an easy condition to live with, and all of the treatments will require regular follow-ups, blood tests and appointments. It will be up to you to manage it all.'

If my world had pivoted slightly after the endometriosis diagnosis two months earlier, now it swung violently. Crohn's would no doubt be more devastating in its severity, duration and impact on my daily life, and if my anxiety was moderate before this development, it ratcheted right up afterwards.

This isn't unusual. Research suggests patients with Crohn's or colitis are twice as likely to have generalised anxiety disorder at some point in their lives. My experience of living with Crohn's was akin to contracting Bali-belly, except without the nice holiday to Bali and without relief, because it stuck around. Everyone responds differently to the various medical treatments for Crohn's, so there wasn't – and there still isn't – a one-size-fits-all solution. Rather, the goal is to reduce the inflammation that triggers a person's symptoms.

Steroids and immunosuppressants were the first lines of treatment I was offered, and both delivered a plethora of unpleasant side effects while remaining largely ineffective at relieving my symptoms. It felt like a lose–lose situation. I despised this disease from the minute I learned of its existence. I hated the colonoscopy to have it diagnosed, I hated the anguish it reeked on my abdomen, I hated the medicine it required, the blood tests it demanded, the toll it took. Mostly, I hated that I had it, but I also hated the fact I hated it.

For reasons I can't really explain, I felt that I ought to have been grateful that my health wasn't worse: that I wasn't facing a death sentence and that it seemed major surgery to have part of my bowel removed – a common experience for people suffering from Crohn's – was highly unlikely. I knew there were children and adults far, far, sicker than I was who would have given anything to be saddled with no more than a mere auto-immune disease. I knew all this. But when you've been handed bad news, knowing that it could have been worse isn't enough to make you feel good about it, unless you've experienced 'worse' for yourself – or at least the prospect of worse. Had I been told that three-quarters of my bowel would have to be removed, and had I mentally prepared myself for the severity of that procedure only to be told that the doctors were mistaken and I would simply need a long course of immunosuppressants, perhaps I would have felt a sustained surge of gratitude. Similarly, if I had been misdiagnosed with something truly sinister, a Crohn's diagnosis, by comparison, would have been welcome. But neither of these scenarios played out, so simply knowing 'I was lucky it wasn't worse' didn't render my ill-health any more palatable.

In the space of four months I discovered that both endometriosis and Crohn's had taken my body hostage, and neither were proving particularly amenable to treatment.

Aside from feeling unwell and being unable to trust my body, the worst part was how lonely it made me feel. A few weeks after

I had begun my first course of treatment for Crohn's, I went to a friend's Saturday afternoon birthday drinks. The plan was to relax on her parents' shady back verandah before making our way to either Caxton Street or the Regatta Hotel later on in the evening, as was the well-worn path of Brisbane uni students.

I was living with my best friend Cass at the time, and getting dressed up together before making our way to the drinks felt excitingly familiar. Having boarded together before sharing a flat we had literally gone through this fun ritual a hundred times before. We swapped clothes as we always did and applied make up in tandem before we hopped in my car to meet a group of mutual friends.

Given my new medication I wasn't going to be drinking, but I wasn't concerned that this would impede my enjoyment of the night. After spending what had felt like months in a medical vortex, navigating surgeries and appointments, I was just grateful to be doing something that felt 'normal' and fun.

Walking in, we were greeted with the typical welcome of nineteen-year-old girls: there were squeals, kisses and hugs. After drinks were poured and we'd settled around the table, the conversation quickly turned to the subject of my health.

'G, what's been happening? Cass said it's been pretty full on, you poor thing ...'

'Yeah, it's been a rollercoaster,' I said. 'I was still feeling so bad after the surgeries last year that I was referred to a new doctor. Now I've been diagnosed with this pretty disgusting disease ...'

I stopped as I felt my voice catch. I didn't want to cry. It wasn't that I was embarrassed about my tears – these girls had seen me cry a million times before – but I didn't want to cry about *this*. I didn't want the afternoon to be about my health. My health had been everything for months and I was sick of it.

'Hopefully, though, that might get a bit better now that I've started treatment,' I finished, before quickly changing the subject. I reached across the slatted timber table and grabbed a single strawberry off the platter laden with cheese and crackers, buying myself a few moments of silence.

The conversation flowed on, and twenty minutes later I took myself off to the bathroom. Outside I was holding it together pretty well, but inside I was shattered. I felt so alone. I had hoped that coming out and being sociable would allow me to leave my boring problems at home, but my problems came with me and created a chasm between myself and my friends. Everyone else sitting around that table, a group I had known for years, was having fun, and I was hiding on top of a toilet fighting back tears. I *could* have disclosed my inner torment to the girls on that deck, and I know they would have offered friendship and support and sympathy and understanding. But they couldn't heal the source of my despair. No one could. And that made me feel lonely in a way I never had.

I was conditioned to living with company at that point, having shared my space through boarding school, college and share houses. I rarely spent much time alone and whenever I did I didn't like it. I was – and remain – extroverted. Around other people I found life interesting and full of possibilities. When left to my own devices I inevitably retreated into my own mind, which was far less enjoyable. Being with other people kept my neuroses at bay, which made that day on the deck truly troubling. I'd discovered that it was possible to be surrounded by people I loved and still feel isolated.

The Crohn's was there day and night, creating an impenetrable distance between me and everyone else, which rendered my safety net – the joy I always found in the company of others – less effective. And this was not for lack of trying on the part of friends and family.

The link between loneliness and chronic illness is well known. Doctors have known for years that loneliness has a damaging impact on physical health and longevity, but more recently the opposite has also been found to be true: chronic illness can make you lonelier and for me, it really did.

I was back into the swing of university when the Crohn's diagnosis was confirmed, and the fact that I was feeling so sick so often, that I was unable to predict or trust my body and desperately wanted to act as if none of it was happening, all combined to let the loneliness in. I was torn between needing help and not wanting to need help.

Being unwell wasn't a scenario I relished. I was resentful of my body's failings – in theory and in substance – and to cope I constructed two different worlds: one in which my illness was free to exist, and another for the rest of my life. I was determined that these two worlds should never meet. I would not give in to my illness.

Years later, I would learn about how the toxic tentacles of perfectionism take hold, and it would prove revelatory. As the author and researcher Brené Brown writes: 'Perfectionism is not the same thing as striving to be your best. Perfectionism is the belief that if we live perfect, look perfect, and act perfect, we can minimise or avoid the pain of blame, judgement, and shame. It's a shield. It's a twenty-ton shield that we lug around thinking it will protect us when, in fact, it's the thing that's really preventing us from flight.'

It was the difference between wanting to do well and needing to do well. At school and at university I had always been determined to do well, even without external pressure. I didn't have the weight of anyone else's expectations bearing down on me, and yet I was uncompromising in wielding my own unrealistic expectations over myself. I believed that if I didn't do well, if I failed at something, I would give people a reason to judge me. Doing well was a form of self-protection. I didn't seek to deny or minimise my illness because of a healthy motivation to live a balanced life. I *needed* to deny my illness lest it shatter the shield of perfection I was unknowingly carrying around.

In light of this, it was unsurprising that I reacted badly when my gastroenterologist suggested I reconsider studying law. This was not the gastroenterologist with the sleek rooms – his dismissive manner had prompted me to seek out another specialist. My new specialist's rooms were much more modest, and were attached to a busy Brisbane hospital. I had skipped a lecture to make the appointment across town, and after going through my latest test results and symptoms and tweaking my medication dosage, I was getting ready to leave.

'One more thing, Georgie.' He paused as I hovered by the door. 'In all honesty, law might not be the sensible choice for you,' he said. 'Crohn's disease is exacerbated by stress, and it is something you are going to need to manage for the rest of your life.'

Maybe I imagined it, but his manner in dishing out this advice felt annoyingly imperious.

How would you have liked to have your career plans foiled by a mysterious disease at the age of twenty? is what I wanted to retort.

'At the moment I'm just studying, so maybe by the time I start working I'll be feeling a lot better,' is what I actually said.

His words weren't without merit or compassion, but it wasn't the kind of advice I was seeking and it certainly wasn't advice I wanted to hear. I wanted him to help soothe my erratic stomach, not question the one part of my life that was ostensibly tracking along without drama.

I had grown hostile to medical advice. I treated every indicator that chronic illness might be woven into the fabric of my life with venom, so the suggestion that I should surrender to Crohn's and change courses made me see red. I batted it away and assured him I could manage.

It is impossible not to consider what might have transpired if I had heeded his advice. What if I *had* changed the way I approached my health and wellbeing at that point in time? Would I have circumvented everything that was to come?

I did myself few favours – psychologically – with the manner in which I approached my health. I absorbed each diagnosis as evidence of my catastrophic flaws and was pathologically determined to participate in life as though illness was not an issue. There is no point in denying that. But there were others who contributed.

The gynaecologist was a case in point.

'Georgina, it's quite obvious you wouldn't exactly last a round in a boxing ring, would you?' he said with his eyes boring into mine.

Did I hear him wrong? Did he hear me wrong? Has he mistaken me for another patient? A patient who is a boxer? Why would I want to last a round in a boxing ring?

I could not make sense of the sentence I'd just heard, and when I glanced over at Mum sitting in the chair beside me, the expression on her face suggested I wasn't alone in my confusion. After several long seconds of silence, he continued.

'I mean, really, what I am saying, Georgina, is you have had a few minor procedures and most people bounce back a lot faster than you.'

Ah. Got it. How perfectly humiliating.

It was five days since I'd had my third and final laparoscopy and I was failing to hit the mark in my recovery. Another weakness revealed! Not only had my body taken it upon itself to grow endometrial tissue where it didn't belong, but I was, evidently, unable to cope with the operations to remove it like everyone else could. Was there no end to my shortcomings?

Having never stepped foot in a boxing ring, I wasn't in a position to offer any meaningful comparison but, honestly, after the operations I did feel like I had survived something brutal. And it felt like the man responsible had just punched me in the face as a parting gift.

When we left the appointment to drive home, Mum was furious.

'How dare he say that? You are nineteen and you've just had three operations in five weeks – how else are you meant to feel? Who wouldn't be wiped out?'

'I guess other people are just a bit stronger than me,' was all I could offer.

I couldn't share Mum's fury. This was proof of what I'd already suspected. If I was stronger I wouldn't have these problems. If I was stronger I would bounce back faster from surgery. If I was stronger I wouldn't have been scared of these operations or affected by the pain.

In five weeks I had endured three general anaesthetics for three laparoscopies, and downed myriad painkillers. Before each of these procedures, I had to submit myself to the truly unpleasant rigmarole of a bowel prep, which involves guzzling two litres of the vilest liquid you have ever tasted, over the course of a few hours. This triggers an evacuation of your stomach over the following few hours. Charming, yes? It was horrendous and was made worse by the fact I had to stop eating twenty-four hours before starting each prep and fast until after the procedure. So regardless of how I was feeling beforehand, by the time I got to the hospital to have my abdomen cut open, I was already feeling obliterated.

The first procedure was the worst. Mum had come up to Brisbane the night before and after being 'checked in' to the hospital in the morning, we'd been taken to a little room from which I would be collected at whatever time the schedule allowed. I sat up on the bed, Mum took the hard plastic chair and we chatted while we flicked through a stack of magazines.

The first few hours went by quickly, but as lunchtime came and then went, and I remained uncollected and deliriously hungry, time slowed right down. While part of me was eager to avoid the procedure altogether, now that I was here, I just wanted it to happen. I had fretted enough, I was starving and my patience had faded. Eventually, as it neared 4pm, I was collected, and the adrenaline kicked in quickly as I was poked and prodded by the anaesthetist. I wanted to throw up; my heart thrashed away and my fears escalated into a mad crescendo. I was told to count to ten and I don't remember making it past three.

The next thing I remember feeling was sweet relief.

I made it out alive! I'm still here! I didn't die! I DID NOT DIE!

As operations go, a laparoscopy is minor, but naturally, my mind had been less interested in the objective medical risk than in the minuscule chance that something devastating could occur. I was concerned I would die – or worse, remain awake for the procedure. In the days leading up to the first procedure, the only thing I had been able to visualise was me, lying on a metal operating table, feeling my abdomen being cut open and being unable to tell anyone I was awake. I became convinced this was a premonition: a subconscious precursor to that scenario playing out. I knew how ridiculous it sounded. Realising I had been wrong had never felt so good. (An upside of being a perpetual worrier is the relief you feel when you realise your worst fears have, in fact, been baseless. Sadly, it never lasts long, because as soon as one worry is eradicated, another worry, or three, pop up in its place.)

Oh dear god, I am alive! I can eat! … but, sweet Jesus, what has happened?

The next phase of coming to was far less pleasant with every minute that passed: giddy relief wore off along with the pain killers and revealed the extent of my body's trauma. The sharp pain of the operation, the discomfort of being connected to various tubes and needles, and the medication-inspired nausea conspired in one awful Molotov cocktail.

Beforehand, I had been warned that the most painful part of my recovery would most likely not be in the three little cuts made to access my pelvis, or in the spot where the trespassing tissue had been cut away, but, rather oddly, in my shoulders.

In laparoscopic surgery, carbon dioxide is pumped into the stomach to distend the abdomen, which irritates the diaphragmatic nerves, which then refers pain upwards through nerve connections, eventually landing in – and aggravating – the shoulder.

To me, it felt like a handful of unforgiving anarchists were having a knife-fight in my upper rib cage. It persisted without relief for forty-eight hours, at which point my extremely tender mid-section took over as my primary grievance. Minor or not, recovering from the laparoscopy was not pleasant or easy. And just as I began to feel close to recovered, a week or so later, it was time to submit myself to the whole thing again. The next two procedures were not without a cumulative toll as the same physical wounds were re-opened. Each time I came away feeling worse than the time before.

So the medico casting aspersions over my not-yet-bounced-back state wasn't exactly fair. In hindsight, his comments were unnecessary at best and cruel at worst. And yet his words – and the sentiment – held.

Five years later, another gynaecologist would offer a very different perspective. I was living in Sydney at that point and because I was still enduring considerable pelvic pain, my GP had referred me to a specialist at St Vincent's in Darlinghurst. He was warm and kind, and seemed to be listening particularly intently as I explained the procedures I underwent when I was first diagnosed with endometriosis.

'You say you had three separate procedures?'

'Yes, three laparoscopies.'

'Over five weeks?'

'Yes. From November to December of 2001.'

'Look I don't want to upset you but operating on a person three times in five weeks is ridiculously unnecessary. I don't know who this cowboy thinks he is but frankly it's disgraceful to put anyone through that. I can't believe you had that done to you.'

I was speechless. Perhaps I wasn't as weak as I had thought? Perhaps these procedures had rattled me not because I was deeply flawed or weak, but because the process was legitimately torturous? By then my state of mind was too far gone to change on any point, but still, his words planted a seed that would, with time, grow.

Some serendipity

January 2005

In early 2005 my world pivoted again but this time, thankfully, not on account of a medical diagnosis. It was a chance introduction that might never have happened if it wasn't for another chance meeting a decade earlier. The latter event, which eventually made way for the former, took place in a maths class, on the first day of Grade Seven at high school in Lismore, when the boy in the seat across from me introduced himself. Our new teacher, Mr Layton, had assigned us all seats in a peculiar formation of rows where no desks touched, and asked us to make ourselves familiar with our new neighbours. The classroom quickly erupted with the energy, chatter and laughter of twenty-seven thirteen-year-olds, hot and excited after lunch. There were only a handful of students I knew from my primary school, but lots of the kids knew each other.

I hadn't ever met the tall boy to my left, who had reached his hand out for me to shake, introducing himself as Stuart, but my first impression was that he was friendly and frighteningly neat. He took more care arranging his pencil case, glasses case and notebook on his desk than I had ever seen anyone take. His hair was just as tidy as his desk, as were his uniform and school bag. Everything about him was so perfect that I couldn't help but reach out and move his notebook slightly off centre, sensing it would rattle him. He rolled his eyes, I laughed and we clicked from that moment on.

We bonded over the fact each of us found the other one thoroughly hilarious and we had complementary skill sets. In home economics, his eye for detail and capacity for neatness made him excel at sewing projects, so he completed them for both of us while I did our cooking. In woodwork I designed while he built. Perfectly.

We became so close that our families began spending time together often and remain great friends today. Even after I headed to boarding school, Stu and I stayed in touch and caught up regularly in all of our school holidays. At twenty-two, while I was about to start my last year of university and Stu was halfway through medicine at university in Sydney, he introduced me to a friend of his.

We were in Yamba, an idyllic spot on the north coast of New South Wales. It was just after 5pm in the first week of January, and I had come up to the locally famed Pacific Hotel, perched over the main beach, for a late-afternoon drink with my brother and dad. The pub buzzed as drinks were poured and glasses clinked. A sliding door to the small verandah off the hotel was left wide open, so the sea breeze could cut the humidity. I could occasionally hear the sound of crashing waves over the holiday-makers.

We joined a big table of mutual friends where Stu was making introductions, and a curly-haired boy diagonally opposite me caught my eye. He was tanned, tall and impossibly-fit looking. He stood up to shake hands with my dad and my brother and he grinned at me with smiling eyes as we shook hands. Something clicked.

My family had spent every summer in living memory in Yamba. Various relatives on my mum's side of the family have houses there and a tradition has held over four generations of converging there through late December and early January. Nick had done the same with his family for almost as many years, but until this day, we hadn't met.

Years earlier, and unbeknownst to him, my sister Belinda and I had dubbed him the 'boxer short boy' on account of a pair of board shorts he wore for several successive summers that looked a lot like boxer shorts. We didn't know him, but Yamba is a small place and my assessment, year after year, was that he was rather fond of himself. He was so good-looking that it was the only reasonable conclusion. Thanks to the Yamba grapevine, I knew that in addition to studying medicine in Sydney he was a talented athlete who had played rugby for Australia: clearly the ultimate jock. I was undeterred from that view even when Stu became friends with him and insisted I'd like him.

Upon having my first proper conversation, albeit broken and across a table, with the smiley-eyed jock, I realised Stu had been right. I did like him.

'What brings you to Yamba?' he asked.

'I come every year. Our whole extended family come here every summer, so right now I'm related to almost every person in this postcode'

He laughed. 'I better behave in that case.'

Our conversation could not have been less consequential, but there was chemistry and an immediate attraction that I realised wasn't one-sided when Nick wrangled an invitation to the dinner we were all on our way to. Over dinner with the five members of my immediate family, the man my sister was about to marry and the four members of Stu's family, Nick and I chatted for most of the night.

(Stu has long joked that we'll always owe him for playing Cupid, and it's hard to disagree.)

Nick was everything I hadn't expected him to be. Thoughtful, humble, kind, funny and a voracious reader. He was, to me, a wonderful enigma who I soon dubbed the Big Friendly Giant after the Roald Dahl novel (albeit far more handsome than Quentin Blake's famous illustrations). Later I learned that he found me 'interesting': he deduced from our first meeting that I had a life of my own and was unlikely to play second fiddle to anyone, which he liked.

We spent the first few months of 2005 talking on the phone around the clock, me in Brisbane, him in Sydney. We stole time together whenever we could between our respective study commitments and jobs, and his rugby schedule. There were road trips between Lismore and Murrurundi, a small town in the Upper Hunter where his family lived, a few weekends in Sydney, some mini breaks in Brisbane and hours and hours and hours on the phone. I came to discover that boxer-short boy was quite something.

In some ways we were, and remain, alike. We were both driven and independent, but also light-hearted with a similar outlook on life. We were both eager to work hard but believed that without friends, family and fun in between, the hard work would have no context.

Despite our similarities in one critical regard we could not have been any more different: Nick was as hardwired to believe in himself as I was hardwired to doubt myself. The idea of occupying a mind that repeatedly offered reassurance and encouragement was perplexing and magnetic to me. To him, my capacity to cast doubt on my every ability was equally fascinating.

About six months after we started seeing each other, while I was back home in Lismore, studying for my final exams, a parcel arrived for me. At the time I was in far from perfect health: my Crohn's had been flaring up, so I was thin and weak, and I was still suffering from pelvic pain on a fairly regular basis. Over the course of the many, many hours we had spent talking, I had revealed to a lot Nick about my medical history. Not all in one go, but gradually, drip by drip. When the full extent of my ailments became obvious to him, I remember us both laughing about it. I'd said it would certainly be useful to have medical advice in-house.

I opened the envelope and caught a glimpse of the printed title: 'A Medical History'. He had prepared a medical report of sorts based on my history that included everything I had ever told him about my health: it had a timeline, a list of every medication I had ever taken, every procedure I had undergone, the different doctors I had seen, their diagnoses and recommendations, and it was all laid out in one handy document. Admittedly this was not conventionally romantic correspondence, but it made me cry – with sadness and relief. I had an ally.

Luck is fickle and often gets more credit than it deserves, but when it comes to finding love, it can't be dismissed. Luck alone might not sustain relationships, but there is fate at play when you find a person who happens to light your world in the same manner you seem to light theirs. In meeting Nick, I got lucky. (The fact that his enthusiasm, energy and optimism are Herculean has proved to be another great stroke of luck.)

Our union hasn't been without hiccups, hostilities, challenges and serious troughs: in myriad ways we quite literally drive one another mad, and our relationship takes work, but virtually from the moment we met, it was a given we'd do life together.

Despite the fact we were young, lived in separate states and juggled different lives, being together felt easy. When I was offered a graduate legal position in Sydney, it seemed it would become even easier: we would finally be in the same place.

I arrived in Sydney in the first week of February 2006. Nick and I had decided that it would be too much to move in together straight away, so I moved into a rental terrace in Darlinghurst with four other girls I knew from Brisbane and he flatted a few suburbs away with two friends. All of my roommates had migrated from Queensland for the same reason: they had finished university and been offered jobs in the Emerald City. Two of us were due to start in law firms, two were headed into banks and the other was working as a nurse while also studying.

Even better, my graduate position wouldn't start till August: I'd have a glorious six months of freedom before it was time to get serious about my work. Then, a week after I'd arrived in Sydney, I received a phone call from the firm I was set to work for.

As fate would have it, I was doing some nannying work that day, wrangling the children of a corporate lawyer and her stockbroker husband. Trying to keep a one-year-old baby and three-year-old twins alive meant I missed a call from my employer-to-be. It wasn't until several hours later, when all three kids were finally napping, that I ducked to the kitchen and hit play on the voicemail. 'Hi Georgie, this is Abigail,' it began. 'We spoke last year about your contract, and the reason I am calling is that we have had some changes and there is actually now an opening for a graduate lawyer in the February intake. If it's possible we'd love you to start earlier. Can you please give me a call when you get this so we can have a chat?'

I felt a rush of adrenaline which may have been rooted in fear or hope, or both. I couldn't tell.

Next week! Is that possible? What about taking a breather? Is this what you want?

I called Nick immediately. 'Isn't the sooner you start, the better?' he asked. 'What do you think?'

'I'm just not sure. I mean I think starting sooner probably makes sense … but it's so soon,' I said. 'I think I have to take it, though. If I don't, maybe they won't think I'm committed?'

'It's up to you. I suppose if you want to do it, you may as well start as soon as you can.'

I returned the call and said I would love to start in February, and the baby woke up before I could think too much more about it. That afternoon, the family's night nanny emerged from the bedroom downstairs, adjacent to the twins' room, and clocked on in time to pick up the family's eldest daughter from school. Together we set about feeding and bathing the four kids, and even with two sets of hands it was excruciating. The oldest child was beside herself, constantly running off to dial her mum's work number, which the nanny had been instructed to forbid. She sobbed and sobbed each time we prevented her from dialling. The nanny explained this was common. Eventually the little girl's sadness turned to rage: she raced into the kitchen, grabbed the set of family car keys from the bench and then hurled them over the back deck beyond the fence that separated their house from the dense national park behind. There was no way we could retrieve them.

The children's father arrived home at 7.30pm. 'We spend over $120,000 a year on nannies and childcare,' he said, almost with pride. 'We have to, though, it's the only way we can both work the way we need to.'

I had babysat and nannied throughout university, but I had never encountered a household quite like this. I left feeling uneasy.

When I arrived back at Darlinghurst that night, my housemates were sitting on our couch near the entranceway. I immediately got them up to speed with the details from my strange day and was so distracted with my storytelling that I almost forgot that my contract had been couriered to me. Seeing a large envelope propped up on our small dining table reminded me of the day's other major development. I opened the paperwork and took a minute to take in the contents of the contract before I signed the dotted lines, ready to send back the following morning.

My grown-up life, my actual career, was about to start. Whatever unnerving vision of the future I had gleaned from my day with the children of a corporate lawyer and high-flying stockbroker was pushed aside.

Graduate positions in law firms are highly coveted. They pay well, they cover the cost of being admitted as a solicitor in your first year, and it's the resume equivalent of a High Distinction on your academic record. Towards the end of the first semester in my second year of law, I'd noticed that the older students were all arriving to lectures and tutorials in suits. It took very little digging to discover the reason: it was interview season. It was my first glimpse of the professional world beyond university and the more I learned about the process, the more determined I grew to land myself one of these positions. Being offered a job by a top tier firm seemed prestigious: an accolade I wanted.

To my surprise I had finished my first year of law with a mix of Distinctions and High Distinctions. I couldn't say that it had always been my dream to be a lawyer. In fact, I'd always dreamed of being a journalist, and I had majored in communications with the vague thought that I might someday pursue that dream. But at university I discovered, against the odds, that I *loved* studying law – the intense reasoning it required, the light it shed on the various systems that govern all our lives, its application to daily life – it was all deeply satisfying. And it seemed, inexplicably, that I was good at it. Better than I was at my communications subjects. It seemed the decision had been made for me, and so I set my sights on a future in law.

The recruitment process for corporate law firms is elaborate, and I set about learning everything I possibly could about it. I knew all the key dates, what you needed on your CV to get noticed, which firms hosted events as screening interviews and how clerkships were awarded.

A clerkship is like a paid internship: it can vary from three weeks to three months and basically gives law students a taste of life inside a firm, and the firm a taste of the person behind the university grades. A Distinction grade point average is widely accepted as the minimum to get you into a top-tier firm. Closer to a Credit is tolerated if you are particularly outstanding in other areas – if you play high-level sport or are making serious inroads towards saving the world in your spare time.

I first applied for a clerkship a year too early and, despite getting an interview with a particularly alluring firm, I was not offered a spot. This rejection came a few weeks after my boyfriend at the time had broken up with me, and it's safe to say I was more than a little sensitive to rejection. I knew the offers were usually only given to students in their penultimate year of study, but I was still inconsolable.

It took three days before I could muster the strength to call the firm and ask for feedback. I was reassured that I was a promising candidate who had scored well in the interview, and that had I been in my penultimate year I would most certainly have received a clerkship.

The following year it became clear my fears had been misplaced. I was offered three clerkships at three firms, and the experiences at each were wildly different. My first clerkship took place in the three-week winter break between semesters. The students I worked with were down-to-earth, we were treated to various activities and lunches and seminars, and I liked the work. At the end I was offered paralegal work two days a week for the rest of the year, and the year after. Nothing was guaranteed, but a graduate offer was looking more than likely.

The next was with a much bigger national firm that only had a very small practice in Brisbane at the time. It meant there were only four of us doing the clerkship together, and fewer organised activities and opportunities to be exposed to different practice groups. It was a perfunctory and forgettable experience that I only came to look on with fondness after my next role.

My final clerkship couldn't have been more different from the earlier two, and I remain grateful it wasn't my first taste of life inside a commercial law firm. The practice group I was assigned had been last on my list of preferences, which struck me as quite odd. Odder still, the exact same thing had happened to my good friend Sam with whom, by chance, I was doing the clerkship.

The mystery was solved the minute we arrived. As I shook the senior partner's hand, he said, 'I pick my clerks from the photos, and I have to say, Georgie, you actually look better in real life than in the shot, which is always pleasing.'

I realised, with horror, that he wasn't joking. When I had arrived at my first interview for this firm back in May, in my stiff, never-been-worn-before suit, the receptionist had immediately taken a polaroid photo. She did the same for all of the candidates when they first arrived, attaching them to our resumes – no doubt to jog the memories of the interviewing panels when it came to making their selection. And also, it appeared, to help some partners 'choose' their vacation clerks.

That explained why I was in a practice group I had very little interest in. Over the next month, the shocks kept coming. The same partner, in front of clients and other legal staff, asked whether I would sleep with him. He was married with children and, at a guess, at least double my age. A junior lawyer intervened, which is not insignificant in itself, and suggested the partner's comments weren't appropriate. He was told to be quiet.

'As if you don't want to sleep with her too,' was the retort.

Appealing as the request was, I declined. The public setting at least made it easier to brush off: it was as outrageous as it was offensive. But it certainly wasn't the last inappropriate comment that Sam or I were subject to throughout the four-week program. Would we like to go back to his place for a spa, naked? Did we know how much he looked forward to seeing our faces each day? How much he enjoyed admiring our bodies? Our clothes? Would I consider moving into his home as an ornament?

Daily, Sam and I thanked our lucky stars that at least we were in this together. It was humiliating, but having each other made it less intimidating, and we felt less vulnerable. It didn't take us long to discover we weren't alone either: many young female clerks had been subject to the same behaviour before us and, I can only assume, many more after.

In law firms, partners are kings and summer clerks are barely even pawns. Saying anything even remotely disparaging of a partner is akin to career suicide, even for established senior lawyers. It's an oxymoron for a summer clerk, because you don't even have a career to ruin. Despite this, Sam and I decided we could not, in good faith, say nothing about this partner's conduct. We tentatively raised his behaviour with HR in a group feedback session at the end of the program, and their reaction put us firmly back in our place.

'Girls, it's clear you arrived here wanting to have fun and it seems that's exactly what you got.'

I sat, stunned. *We got what we wanted?*

The underlying message was clear: if anything inappropriate had happened, we had obviously taken part in it willingly. It was as extraordinary to me then as it is now. I am still angry, and disappointed that I wasn't braver or more willing to fight it, but I felt I had little choice.

Fortunately, I was offered a job elsewhere, so what I was subjected to at that firm didn't ruin my life or my career. But it very well could have. The way that partner behaved, and the way the firm responded to our complaint, made it clear that the rhetoric about law firms being bastions of moral conduct, committed to building harmonious work environments, was just that: rhetoric.

I knew that particular partner's behaviour was an aberration rather than the rule, and so too the response from HR, but I wasn't so naive that I believed bad behaviour would never be tolerated in other firms. The confidence about my career path that I'd felt on finishing university was being shaken. For a brief moment I flirted once more with the idea of pursuing a career in journalism. It had always been my dream job, after all … but it wouldn't work. Compared to law, there were so few jobs available, and I had achieved far better marks in my law subjects. Besides, I couldn't give up now, when I had already come so far.

I was determined to make it work.

A hellish harbour view

February 2006

'Look, some people might say he *is* a little bit intense, but he is an absolute genius,' the HR manager said between sips of her white wine, not sounding entirely certain. 'You're really, *really* lucky to be able to work with someone so smart.'

There was a disconnect between the words she was saying and her facial expression: her eyes were drilling into me intensely, like a warning.

Confused, I managed to get out some version of the words that would slip off the tongue of any graduate practised in the art of recruitment: 'I'm sure it will be a fabulous challenge and I'm so grateful for the opportunity.'

It was a sticky afternoon in February and I was sitting on the verandah of the Paddington Bowls Club in Sydney with a group of my new colleagues-to-be. There were ten recent graduates, just like me, a smattering of lawyers a few years ahead of us who were to be our 'buddies' and some representatives from the HR team. The venue, as well as the absence of any partners – and the inevitable pressure their presence would entail – made the event as close to casual as any work function could be. Our real lives, our careers proper, were set to commence on Monday in a tower near Circular Quay, a place with unspoiled harbour views, walls adorned with tasteful art – some of which was worth several of our comfortable starting salaries put together – in-house catering and all the trappings you would expect in a prestigious corporate law firm.

And I had just been told that my boss-to-be, a partner who headed up the division of the firm that I would be joining for my first six-month rotation, might be tricky.

I was uneasy, and it wasn't just because my timeline to commence this job had, just last week, been brought forward by half a year. I'd assured the HR manager that I was looking forward to the challenge, mostly because I knew they were the words she wanted to hear. They were the words I wanted to say, the words I wanted to believe, but as I took a sip from my own glass of wine, I was aware they weren't true. Not even close.

Almost anyone who has done any work inside a large law firm will have a tale or two about a tyrannical partner. These men and women are feared and revered in equal measure: they are not afraid of throwing phones and think nothing of publicly dressing down members of their team, they expect an immediate response to every email regardless of the time it's dispatched, and generally have everyone in their vicinity living on a knife's edge.

They are, usually, oblivious to the chaos they wreak, and they remain firmly ensconced in the employ of whichever firm they find themselves in, because in addition to being badly behaved, these men and women are usually celebrated rainmakers: they bring in so much revenue that their sins are forgiven, and their poor behaviour is accepted as an unfortunate side effect of brilliance.

I had already seen enough of these tyrants in action to know their existence wasn't mere hearsay, and the idea of being at the whim of one of them for my first rotation only added to my unease, which had been building since the second I walked into the bowls club. All the other graduates seemed to know one another well, having either studied at the same Sydney universities or completed a clerkship at the firm together. Fresh from Brisbane, I was the only newbie. On top of that, university lore had it that graduates who got positions at top-tier firms in Sydney were the best of the best: in the hierarchy of firms and the hierarchy of cities, these young men and women were the anointed ones, and I wasn't convinced that I belonged in that category. Brisbane wasn't as competitive as Sydney, I reasoned, so it must have been easier for me to get through. I probably got the job as a favour, as a mistake or a lucky break.

Beneath all these worries was a more troubling one that I couldn't ignore, hard as I tried: I wasn't sure that I actually wanted this job at all, the job I had worked doggedly towards for the past six years.

This is what you wanted! You barely drew breath during your course to get here, so what's the problem?

I had to push it away. The fact I succeeded in doing that was thanks to my peers who – guys and girls alike – struck me as being straightforward and sincere. As I left, Annie, a curly-haired girl with a huge smile and an infectious laugh, who I had sat beside for most of the event, grabbed my hands. 'We're going to be friends, Georgie, I can tell. And we're going to survive! Promise!'

BREAKING BADLY

I left that evening thinking that solidarity and friendship were going to matter. I just didn't know how much.

~

To: Georgina Dent
From: Tanya
Subject: Missing timesheets

Georgina

We are missing your timesheets for the past fortnight. Please complete and return ASAP.

Tanya

To: Tanya
From: Georgina
Subject: Re Missing timesheets

Hi Tanya

This is my first day at the firm so I don't have any timesheets to fill out. I will complete and return my timesheet for this week on Friday.

Many thanks
Georgie

To: Georgina Dent
From: Tanya
Subject: Re Re Missing timesheets

I still need them.

Tanya

Okay ... this was a little tricky. Tanya was the executive assistant to the partner and two senior associates in this division. Twenty minutes earlier she'd knocked at my office door and looked startled to see me, even though we had been introduced just a few hours earlier.

'Where is David?' she'd asked without a flicker of recognition.

'I am Georgie, the new graduate ...' I said. 'David has moved downstairs and rotated into a new group.'

Her face was blank. 'Well, this is for David,' she said as she passed a client's file over. 'He needs this.'

'No trouble, I will take care of it,' I said, taking the thick manila folder from her hands.

I looked up David's new extension on the firm's intranet, rang him and then delivered the files to the relevant senior associate, as he instructed. That exchange was odd enough, but *this* – being chased for time-sheets when I hadn't even been an employee – was stranger still. I stared at my screen, re-read Tanya's emails, and fought the urge to bang my head on the desk.

Timesheets, the bane of lawyers' working lives, are hideous forms in which you must account for your working day in six-minute blocks known as 'billable units'. Every six minutes of your working day needs to be identified and recorded – what you did, who you can charge for it, who instructed you to do it – and every lawyer has a daily target of billable time to meet to ensure they are profitable. The process and the forms are godawful and have been linked to the high rates of depression among lawyers for the mindset they promote.

Aside from rewarding inefficiency and being a woeful indicator of value, being at the mercy of a timesheet is akin to being slowly suffocated. Every non-billable activity you undertake during waking hours – a bathroom break, a firm-wide meeting, chatting to a colleague – feels illicit and wanton and wasted. *BACK TO WORK* the timesheet is always screaming.

I knew timesheets were part of the deal, but surely I wasn't expected to complete one for days when I hadn't even been employed yet?

I opened the billing software, clicked on the 'add entry' button to fill out the forms and completed the whole calendar month before today. I allocated eight hours of non-billable time to the task of being 'Not yet employed' every day of the previous month. It did the trick, because half an hour later a new email icon flashed up on my screen, and when I opened it I saw a two-word message from Tanya: *Thank you.*

It was all very strange, but I felt buoyed by the fact I had managed to avoid getting an important gatekeeper offside. Partners' executive assistants rank high above almost everyone else, but particularly juniors like me. They usually know the place back to front and are valuable allies. Treating EAs with disdain is a serious mistake from which many junior lawyers do not recover, so I was thrilled to have avoided one major pitfall.

The office that now had my name on the door was small but boasted a direct view of the Opera House, the Harbour Bridge and Circular Quay in all of its glistening glory. As I took it in, I felt a rare rush of satisfaction. My new boss was going to be away for my whole first week, but the rest of the team couldn't have been more welcoming. I was taken out for lunch, brought up to speed on the work I would be doing and taken through the main pieces of legislation I would need to refer to. I was prepped around client and firm etiquette – the version not discussed in formal training sessions. There were still a few orientation sessions with the new grads to come, which would give me regular opportunities to touch base with my allies and get to know them all a little bit better.

As the week went on I noticed a theme. From what I could piece together, gathering information from the files I was working on, the outdated name tags on office doors and comments made by new colleagues, it seemed a lot of staff had exited this group in recent times. But my first week had been perfectly pleasing. My days were manageable, and I felt like I was getting a handle on how my life as a lawyer would pan out.

The second week was very different.

'Ah, Hamish, how was your weekend?' one of my senior colleagues said to my new boss as he snaked his way from the lift lobby to his office.

'FAIR TO GOOD, OKAY!' a voice spat back.

I heard this exchange from my office, which was tucked around the corner, but it was enough to make my stomach lurch.

Hamish wasn't back three hours before he insisted that I move to an office closer to his. This had been predicted by my peers the week before – apparently he liked the junior to always be within earshot. So I reluctantly left behind my beautiful view and set up in the cubicle next to his, noting, grudgingly, that thanks to his habit of yelling everything, I would have been able to hear him just as well from my old office. At least, unlike my previous unpleasant boss, Hamish's desire for proximity was not lewd (though he would come to boast to me of his illicit moment of affection with another married member of staff). He just wanted to ensure his lackey could respond to his barks as quickly as possible.

It is impossible to recount this period in my life without regret. At the time I did not, for a single moment, consider myself vulnerable, but in reality I was twenty-three years old and had been thrown like a lamb to the slaughter. The man I worked for had had nine members of staff leave in the six months before I joined – and it was a team of six. He went hot and cold, and was aggressive, void of self-awareness and really difficult to please. Even with all the warnings, I hadn't been prepared for the daily reality of working with a 'genius'.

<u>To: Georgina</u>
<u>From: Hamish</u>
<u>Subject: Client Correspondence</u>

WRONG GEORGINA. WRONG!!!

Oh faaaaarrrrrrkkk …
Five minutes earlier, he'd summoned me and asked that I send an email to a client with two documents attached. Oddly, the time it took him to ask me and then send me an email with the relevant documents was longer than it would have taken to simply complete the task himself, but this wasn't exactly out of the ordinary.

I tried to think of what I could possibly have got wrong: he'd sent the two documents to me himself so I knew they were the attachments he wanted included, and I had the client right because he had given me the name and email address.

How? What the hell did I get wrong?

I stood up and walked to his office, tail between legs, but I was waved away: he was too angry to look at me. Fifteen minutes later he responded to the email I sent the client – which he was copied in on – and began his response: 'Please disregard the previous email from my junior.'

He then proceeded to provide a few hundred words of legal advice that I could not possibly have written, because I couldn't possibly have known it. It was starkly beyond my expertise.

I was sure I hadn't done anything wrong, but the fact remained I couldn't do anything right.

I may not have been the most physically and mentally robust 23-year-old when I started working as a lawyer, but nor was I particularly strung out, frazzled or in need of an intervention. Slowly, that seemed to be changing. I cried more often than I ever had – in the bathrooms, in the park opposite our building, in the offices of other staff members, in the lobby downstairs. But never, I believe, in front of Hamish.

Maybe this was just what being a lawyer was like? Maybe I just needed to tough it out until my skin had thickened? Sure, I was working a lot of hours, which didn't help with the crying situation. I'd done a few all-nighters, and there were whole weeks when I hadn't got to bed before 2am and was back at my desk before 8am the next morning, but this was not out of the ordinary. In a corporate division, it's deals that dictate how and when you work, and many lawyers consider all-nighters a badge of honour. But for me, coupled with Hamish's constant demands and impossible expectations, it came at a cost.

A few months before my sister was due to get married, her future in-laws were due to visit Sydney from Townsville on a weekend when my parents would also be in town, so they decided to meet up for dinner on the Friday night at an Italian restaurant in Leichhardt. It was the first time I would meet my brother-in-law's parents and sister, and I wanted to make the best possible impression.

On the night of the dinner, work dragged and dragged, and I wasn't able to finish until 7pm. Nick picked me up from the office, and as we crawled through the city peak-hour traffic to Leichhardt, I burst into tears.

'Hey, talk to me. What's up?' Nick asked.

'I … I …' I tried to answer between sobs, without any luck.

'Georgie. What's going on?'

'I am terrible at my job and I'm a terrible sister. My boss hates me. Nothing I ever do is right or good enough,' I eventually got out. 'Look, we're turning up an hour late to dinner. We don't even have a gift to take. I just feel so selfish.'

'Darling, it's your family. They understand. They know you. You are never late!'

'It's not the point. They shouldn't have to understand me being late *tonight*. They shouldn't have to handle me being an emotional wreck. Why do I always have to make everything so hard?'

As we pulled up I wiped harshly at my face, hoping that at least I'd got my tears out of the way. No such luck. After apologising profusely, we sat down for approximately thirty seconds before I dissolved in tears and was unable to stop crying for the duration of dinner.

To the credit of everyone at that table, my emotional spectacle was greeted with kindness and various soothing reassurances. The worst thing about that evening was that I really had no good reason to cry. It had been a stressful day, and I had been soundly admonished by Hamish, but these events were par for the course. I couldn't pinpoint a specific trigger for my waterworks, but I also just couldn't make them stop. Why the hell couldn't I cope?

While my mental health was slowly unravelling in the background, there was nothing gradual about my physical problems. Since my diagnosis, I'd mostly been able to manage my Crohn's, but suddenly it seemed to have become worse than ever, forcing me to become something of a regular at the local emergency department and my gastroenterologist's office. My stomach had become completely unpredictable, which meant every meeting, conversation and commute was laden with fear.

So physically I wasn't exactly flourishing, but I didn't know how to overcome these problems and I was determined not to surrender to them. I figured I would just have to fight through it.

Thankfully this became a lot easier once the first six months of my life as a lawyer were over. On the first Monday of my second rotation, I walked in and noticed a handful of the team casually gathered around one of the EAs' desks, laughing together about a disaster that had happened over the weekend. The senior associate had thrown a birthday party for her three-year-old daughter, and the poor little girl had thrown up just as everyone was singing 'Happy Birthday'.

Their ease with one another felt entirely unfamiliar to me. In big law firms, individual practice groups operate like their own countries, with their own cultures and laws. The transition from my first rotation to my second was like escaping World War II Germany and landing in Switzerland. People were kind and respectful and appeared to like each another. There was no yelling. There was camaraderie and smiling. People arrived at work and asked one another about their lives. It was heaven and provided me with some perspective.

In a catch-up session that took place after I had spent about a month in the new group, one of the partners noted a visible change in my demeanour.

'When you first arrived, it seemed like you were on edge,' he said. 'You sat sort of frozen at your computer and practically jumped whenever someone said hello.'

It seemed I was on edge because I was. I *did* jump when someone said hello. It took time, but eventually I did defrost. I came to welcome colleagues arriving at my door to give me work and enjoyed being part of a group of people who genuinely liked and respected one another. My working hours became much more civilised and I even got satisfaction from the work itself. My Crohn's continued to cause trouble, exacerbated by a return of the endometriosis symptoms, but my stress levels had definitely dropped, so I felt confident I could keep control of my physical issues as long as I remained strong.

Eventually, I finished the course, to be admitted alongside my fellow graduates. I began to think that maybe a career in law could work out after all.

The cracks start to show

February 2007

My heart was thumping. Small beads of sweat had formed above my brow and I was flooded with a familiar mix of gratitude and dread. Gratitude because I'd made it. Dread because work was still five minutes away. I was sitting in a cafe bathroom cubicle that I had become familiar with for the worst of reasons: necessity. Frequent necessity. It had become a halfway house on my commute to the office. The bathroom itself, off to the left at the back of the cafe, was always clean and, mercifully, always free. As far as communal bathrooms go it was pleasant, but I hated it.

Arriving bang on peak hour had helped me stay relatively inconspicuous on the way in. To disguise my unease, I'd focused on appearing entirely nonplussed, casually scouting my eyes around the tables as if I was looking for someone while I made my way to the toilet. Now I had to face the outside again. I had to rally.

You are okay. You can do this. You have an upset tummy but you are a professional. Once you get to work you will be fine. You're just thinking too much.

The mental feat of pulling myself together had been taking a little longer with each passing day, but I still prevailed. As always, I strode out of the cubicle with a smile on my face and faith that I *could* do it. On the way out, I deliberately made eye contact with a waiter.

'Thanks, hope you don't get too hot in here today!' I said lightly. Nothing to see here! Just a junior corporate type visiting the bathroom.

The charade was for my own benefit. Pretending that what had just happened hadn't happened was the only way I could get myself to the office.

Three weeks earlier, at the end of January, Nick and I had bid our respective share houses farewell and moved into a tiny art deco studio apartment in Darlinghurst. It felt novel and grown-up to be cohabiting. Setting up our compact unit together was a bright spot in what had become a rather dark time, because I was constantly unwell.

In November I'd taken two weeks off work to have another operation in an unsuccessful bid to settle my implacable abdomen. At this point it was difficult to distinguish whether the pain, purging, twisting and cramping that accompanied my every day were being caused by Crohn's, endometriosis or both. It was decided that a procedure to eliminate endometrial tissue from the equation was warranted, to be performed by the gentle surgeon who had described my first gynaecologist as a 'cowboy'. It was my fourth procedure of the kind.

The operation was straightforward if not enjoyable. After subjecting myself once again to the indignity of vacating my digestive system in preparation, I was admitted to St Vincent's Private Hospital early one Tuesday morning and had the procedure that afternoon. I stayed in hospital for two nights, with Mum and Nick my trusty companions, and then spent ten days recovering. Knowing what I was in for, having the support and encouragement of a caring doctor and not having to return to the arena for follow-up procedures all meant it was easier in many ways than it was when I was nineteen. But without a robust foundation of good health to return to, I was far from fighting fit by the time I returned to work. I felt terrible that I had inconvenienced the firm and my group by taking sick leave for an operation, especially when, as the days went by, it became clear my symptoms hadn't improved. The fact that my peers were so accommodating and kind actually compounded my guilt: I could hardly blame my physical woes on keeping up with the demands of an unforgiving dictator. So I soldiered on, pretending that I felt better than I did.

The move to our new flat meant that, technically, my daily commute was an easy ten-minute walk from the top of Hyde Park towards Circular Quay, but in reality it was anything but easy. It had become a torturous obstacle course, impossible to complete without at least two bathroom stops, if not three. I came to know the exact location of every bathroom facility between my office and our flat because I had cause to dash to most of them. Often.

I would arrive at the office each morning already wiped out from an invisible war my stomach was fighting, which I dared not mention to anyone, simply because everything about it was mortifying. Cruelly, I had become so fearful of needing to run for the loo at any moment, that needing to run for the loo at any moment was inevitable.

Will I need to use the bathroom? How will I excuse myself? What if I need to excuse myself three times? What will they think is wrong with me? How can I hide this?

I didn't recognise the symmetry then, but in hindsight, just as I was trying to purge the gloom from my head, my body was physically purging everything inside it. I wasn't living in total denial about the tiresome quirks of my digestive system: I was seeing my gastroenterologist regularly and trying new medications. I had cut gluten and sugar from my diet altogether and was taking a variety of different supplements to help. Nothing worked, and the more time went on without any improvement, the more stressed I became about the fact I wasn't improving.

And yet – it's sad but true – the most stressful part of being so unwell wasn't that I felt physically dreadful; it was worrying that my illness would be construed as a sign that I was weak or lazy or difficult.

By this stage I had begun my third and final rotation in the firm, in a litigation department, and despite the team being wonderful, the job wasn't without challenges. One night in the office, just before 7pm, I heard a knock on the door and swung my swivel chair around to see Alfonso, my friend and fellow grad, standing just inside the door.

'How's the day going?' he asked.

That question was almost rhetorical – he'd known the answer before he asked. I was in the thick of a case that was flowing seamlessly from missed deadlines to miscommunications to monumental bungles. It had been a disaster, and while Alfonso wasn't working in the same practice group as me, his office was close enough for him to be familiar with filing dates that had been missed, deadlines that kept getting moved, work being duplicated and tensions running high.

'I think I'll be able to bill *something* at least!' I laughed while rolling my eyes. 'What about you?'

'I actually got some positive feedback from that memo I drafted.'

'Truly?'

'Yup.'

These kinds of debriefs had become something of an evening ritual for us, exchanging war stories from the day. Alfonso was familiar with the angst that comes from having very little control over your days. As the firm's underlings, we operated at the whims of partners, senior lawyers and clients. The higher a person climbs in a law firm the greater autonomy they secure. We were on the bottom rung, which meant no autonomy at all. We were so lowly, in fact, that we were rarely given a glimpse of the 'big picture'. Instead we were often asked to complete tasks without any context, which meant we were regularly blindsided when it came to the next step. Having a substantive task doled out at 5.30pm with a tight turnaround wasn't unusual – in fact it was practically expected. The salt in the wound was when this kind of task was handed to you at the end of a quiet day, after you had been hanging around and asking for work since morning, unsure of how you could possibly meet your billable target without anything to do.

I had just spent the whole of Easter in the office doing what's called 'discovery'. Discovery is where the parties to any legal dispute have to provide each other with all the relevant information and known facts of a case. In corporate insolvency cases involving large companies, this can mean reading through thousands and thousands of emails, memos, letters and contracts, either to or from your client, to ascertain *anything* relevant. Needle in a haystack barely covers it. I spent four twelve-hour days riffling through paperwork, only to be told on the Tuesday morning after the break that the client wasn't going to pay for it. The matter was going to be settled anyway so discovery wasn't necessary. Those hours I'd spent working were to be written off – they weren't 'billable' – putting me behind my target for the month despite having barely left the office.

On this particular evening, as Alfonso stood in my doorway, I was probably more stressed than usual, though my perception of stress had become a little skewed. Ten minutes into our debrief, I stood up from my desk and something strange happened: the world violently tilted off its axis. If someone had told me an earthquake had just struck our building I would have believed them. But, apparently, there was no earthquake: no one else in the office felt the world tremble. It was just me. My office was spinning and I felt woozy, so I lay down on the floor while Alfonso went to get me a glass of water. He returned quickly, along with another friend.

'Are you okay?' Tess asked, kneeling down beside me.

'I don't know,' I said, disoriented. 'I feel awful.'

I sat up and drank some water, but my office continued to spin. Tess helped me downstairs and found a taxi to take me home, all of five minutes away. I climbed up the two flights of stairs to our tiny flat, fumbled my key in the door and made a beeline for our bed. Nick was in Canberra for the night and I knew he'd be at training, so I sent him a quick text to say that I was having an early night and would call him in the morning.

I left the lights off. I couldn't stand the idea of anything bright. Moving in the dim light from the street lamps outside, I left my work clothes in a pile on the floor, pulled on a pair of cotton shorts and an old t-shirt, and fell into bed. I buried my head under the pillow in search of darkness, closed my eyes and hoped to god that this awful sensation would disappear overnight.

~

It didn't. I woke up to the sound of my alarm and realised with a sinking stomach that I felt terrible. The natural light hurt my eyes and I scrambled to remember why my head was pounding.

Did I go out last night?

I sat up in our queen-sized bed and wished there was a glass of water in reach as I slowly registered what felt like the hangover from hell. Everything ached. My brain, my joints, my bones. Everything felt heavy and foggy, and I wanted to lie back down, pull the doona over my head and go back to sleep. As it dawned on me that my wretched state could not be blamed on a late night slamming tequila shots, I wanted to throw up. I remembered falling over. The dizziness. There was no clear reason for feeling like I was.

What the hell is WRONG with you? How many sick days can one person take??

Why can't you just suck it up like everybody else? Are you really so hopeless that you can't handle working?

I managed to get myself in the shower, where I stood motionless under the stream of hot water, blinking back tears, *trying* not to catastrophise. The idea of having to take another sick day was sickening.

You can't! It's not an option. Just pull yourself together and get into the office.

For fifteen minutes I attempted to get myself dressed and ready for work, determined to be at my desk by 8am like all diligent junior lawyers. Even finding clothes felt like a feat, but not because my wardrobe was messy: my brain was. It felt as though the lines of communication between my mind and hands had been cut. Eventually I emerged triumphant and dressed, but I was unsteady on my feet. As I reached up into the kitchen cabinet to get a bowl for breakfast, I stumbled. It was that vertigo again.

To steady myself I held onto the kitchen bench and didn't move. Hoping the dizzy spell would pass, I slowly inched myself across the timber floors and back to bed. I lay down, but my corporate uniform was suffocating. My blouse, skirt and stockings were too stiff and tight. I felt claustrophobic. My heart raced as I realised that I couldn't do it. I couldn't pretend today. Not even here, in my own home.

It was hopeless. No amount of denial could circumvent how I felt. After stripping out of my wretched work clothes, I pulled on a pair of jeans that were soft and comfortable. I conceded defeat and rang the office to say I wouldn't be in. I then rang the medical centre where my GP worked and took the first available appointment for the day. It was with a doctor I hadn't seen before, but it would have to do.

Before I left home I put on a smart jumper, a chic pair of ballet flats, tinted moisturiser, a dab of blush and a lick of lipstick. By the end, I was satisfied that at least I looked far better than I felt. Perhaps, had I seen my regular GP, it might have been more difficult to hide how bad – and fearful – I truly felt. As it was, I didn't tell the unfamiliar doctor that I was increasingly concerned by my worsening Crohn's, or that I was feeling less resilient every day. I didn't say that I cried at the drop of a hat, that I berated myself daily, that I was struggling. I sat up straight, smiled and did my best to give the impression that I really had no idea where this spell of dizziness had come from. At least that was partially true.

This kind of ruse, pretending to be better than I was and projecting an air of nonchalance, was partly ingrained, but it also had a more recent source. The year before, a gastroenterologist had let slip that I was what doctors call a 'heartsinker'. Heartsinkers are the patients who don't respond to treatment as expected, who become overly emotional about their medical problems or don't bounce back quickly. The sight of their name on the daily run sheet is enough to make the treating professional's heart sink. As a pathological people-pleaser, I was horrified to hear this. So I adjusted my behaviour to ensure I wouldn't easily land in that category again. It would be a long time before I recognised how adept I had become at this particular style of manipulation. At the time I might have explained it as simply wanting to communicate clearly and put my best foot forward in any appointment, but the truth is I wanted every doctor I saw to like me. Even if that meant compromising my ability to be treated effectively.

On the basis of the incomplete history I gave the GP, she concluded that the vertigo would likely go away, but suggested I get a CT scan of my head – just in case – and handed me a referral to an ear, nose and throat (ENT) specialist.

'They deal with vertigo all the time,' she said. 'Call to make the appointment as soon as possible because there will be a waiting list. If the dizziness goes away before your appointment you can always cancel it, and if it doesn't go away, you'll need to see him.'

As she walked me to her door she mentioned the name of a man who was super-specialised in the field of vertigo – 'the guru of all things dizzy'. She suggested that in the unlikely event that my symptoms didn't go away easily, it would be worth trying to get an appointment with him. I filed his name away in my mind, hoping I wouldn't have cause to draw on his expertise.

Later that afternoon I got the CT scan done and it came back clear, so I returned to work the next day, still feeling sick. Aside from the physical symptoms, I was embarrassed and self-conscious about having had more time off. In hindsight, I'm sure no one was sufficiently invested in either my presence or absence to justify my mortification, but I felt certain I stood out as a great big giant malingerer.

The dreaded dizziness persisted, so a week and a half later, I took myself off to see the ENT specialist in my lunch break. The doctor, whose rooms were in a small terrace house just down the road from St Vincent's, was a compassionate, gentle fellow in his sixties.

'My inkling is that you are suffering from an inner-ear migraine, which can result in imbalance, headaches and nausea,' he said. 'Your symptoms don't fit the bill for Meniere's disease or labyrinthitis, which are the two most common explanations for vertigo. I'm going to give you a referral for an MRI, just to ensure we aren't missing anything.'

'How are these migraines treated?' I asked.

'Not particularly well unfortunately, but there are things you can do to try and alleviate them. Long days in front of a computer screen don't help,' he said. 'I've heard stories about those big law firms … it's no good. To be honest, I'm not surprised this is happening. I would suggest you take a full week off work to rest.'

I was tempted to tell him he didn't know the half of it, but I just laughed and mentally rewarded myself for being so jovial and likeable.

He won't think I'm a heartsink patient! I laugh at his jokes! I am so laid back!

Beneath this facade, it was *my* heart that was sinking, and my stomach had twisted at the thought of needing more time off.

If you have ever been told by a specialist that you need to take time off work for the vague purpose of relaxing, chances are you might recognise the internal angst this triggered. Taking leave from work in order to rest means having a conversation with someone – the person responsible for your employment, no less – about your inability to cope. This is daunting at the best of times, but it's terrifying when you are desperately trying to hold things together.

I returned to the office feeling glum and defeated, less certain than ever that my work life need not be limited by my physical health. I quickly shot off an email to Mum.

> Hi Ma,
> I just saw the ENT and he thinks the dizziness is from a migraine. Stress related (!) so he wants me to take a week off work. I am thinking I might fly to Ballina on Sunday and come home for the week. Are you and Dad around?
> Love g

> Hi G,
> I have been waiting to hear. Time off for some R & R sounds sensible. Dad and I are around and we'd love to have you – we'll take care of you.
> Love Mum.

I scheduled a meeting with James – one of my bosses and a genuinely lovely man – to explain my predicament. For all the difficult characters in laws firms, there are also some gems, and I had never been as grateful for one of them than I was on that particular day.

There were tears and apologies and promises (all from me) as I updated James on my vertigo.

'Georgie, you just do what you need to do to get better,' he said. 'You being well is what matters.'

I was slowly coming around to that perspective, and in that one short meeting he rendered what I feared was a sackable offence okay.

'Thank you, James,' I said. 'I promise I will be better when I come back.'

I really, really wanted that to be true. I booked flights to Ballina, hopeful that a week away from Sydney, away from the office, in the comfort of my parents' home, would be the tonic my spinning head needed.

~

After a few days with my family, I was keen for a change of scenery. I decided that a day trip to Byron Bay, a forty-minute drive from my parents' home, would help. Even though it was May, it was sunny and warm enough on the north coast to make a day by the beach appealing. Surely time outside in the sunshine couldn't hurt.

The drive was relaxing. The road between Lismore and Byron Bay snakes through beautiful Bangalow and is framed by lush hinterland, opening up to occasional glimpses of coastline. I knew the road, having travelled between Brisbane and home countless times, and there was comfort in its familiarity. The sun was shining, I was taking care of myself and I started to imagine knocking this vertigo on the head.

After turning off the highway towards the centre of town, something changed. By the time I approached the roundabout onto the main street, I was aware that my palms were sweaty and my heart was pumping violently. I tried to keep breathing. I gripped the steering wheel tight, swung the car into the first spot I saw and sat in shock. My hands were shaking, my heart was thumping and the fear was paralysing.

This isn't okay.
This isn't normal.
This isn't okay.
You aren't okay.
This isn't normal.
You aren't normal.

Ten minutes passed before I could bring myself to get out of the car and walk a hundred metres towards to the beach. I spread my beach towel out on the sand and sat down, letting the adrenaline drain from my body. The sun was warm on my face and the water was crystal clear with barely a ripple. The physical surrounds could not have been more idyllic – or further from the un-idyllic landscape of my mind. I breathed and eventually the heart palpitations faded. But my shock remained.

Maybe this week isn't going to heal you.
Maybe a week away from work isn't enough to resolve whatever the hell is happening to you.
Maybe this is just you now.
Maybe you can't do this.

I felt like I was perched on a precipice and didn't know how to get down. I felt stuck.

~

I approached my mission to de-stress as if it were an assignment I could knock over with purpose and direction. Each morning after Mum and Dad headed off to work, I set about trying to relax, confident that the dizziness would disappear just as soon as I reached an appropriate state of Zen. Unsurprisingly, my almost manic attempts to unwind yielded nothing even remotely resembling Zen. Effectively, I attempted to yell myself into a state of relaxation, which worked in much the same way as yelling, 'Don't touch that doughnut!' at a child (or yourself). It only ever makes them (or you) want to devour the doughnut more than ever.

Reading a book was impossible because I couldn't get more than a few pages without slipping into the same old thoughts.

Why are you reading a book when you should be at work? You aren't supposed to enjoy yourself. You are supposed to just stop stressing. Why are you reading? You should REST!

Napping was impossible for the same reason.

Why are you trying to sleep in the middle of the day? How lazy can you be?! You should be reading!

I tried focusing on Sudoko puzzles, with limited success – though at least it did distract me for slightly longer than anything else. I couldn't even look at the TV remote without also determining that I was a lazy, indulgent, unproductive member of society who didn't deserve to be entertained.

Even just thinking back to those days makes my skin crawl. There is nothing as stressful, in my experience, as desperately willing an anxious, addled, wound-up mind to switch off. The idleness of those days heightened my panic, and the fact I was out of my routine really threw me. Neither my body nor my mind was able to switch off on cue, so I became increasingly stressed about de-stressing.

Even by this stage, I worried less about my state of health than about the fact I was having time off work. The idea I that *needed* to be better by Friday so I could return to Sydney and be back on deck for the following Monday was looming at all times.

The week drew to a close, and not only did I not feel any better, I actually felt worse. The dizziness, which was accompanied by weakness, heart palpitations, nausea and headaches, persisted, and I felt depleted and lost.

What am I supposed to do? What if I feel like this forever?

Mum and Nick separately murmured about me needing to take stock. There were gentle prods and suggestions that I take a step back to look at the big picture, that I take time out:

'No job is worth your health.'

'Maybe anxiety is an issue?'

'Perhaps a proper break is needed to get your Crohn's back under control?'

'Is corporate law possibly not the best career choice for you?'

These were valid points I was unwilling to properly consider.

To my mind, following their suggestions would amount to me failing and falling short, and I couldn't contemplate that. I clung to the idea that everybody else could manage their lives and careers without falling apart so I could too, and I resented Mum and Nick for doubting me. I stubbornly refused to entertain the idea of asking for more time off work or calling the ENT for an urgent appointment. Instead I returned to Sydney and attempted to proceed with life as normal. I was still desperate to find an explanation for the dizziness, and I was certain that the answer was out there. I just needed to hunt it down.

I remembered that the GP who I had seen the morning after my very first vertigo attack had mentioned a 'guru for all things dizzy', and contacting this specialist went straight to the top of my list. The Guru was a highly regarded neurologist whose practice was renowned for treating people suffering problems with balance and vertigo, and his name was mentioned to me many times in those first weeks of dizziness. However, it turned out that appointments with him were hard to get. There wasn't even a phone number to call. The only way to schedule a sought-after slot was for my doctor to send a letter of referral to his rooms via the post. His rooms would then, at some point, send a fax with an appointment back to the doctor, who would then let me know. There were no negotiations about time – you simply got the time you were given. When we finally received word, my appointment was months away.

So while I waited, I tried other options. I saw an osteopath who thought the vertigo might be structural. I saw another GP who thought a vitamin or mineral deficiency could be at play. I saw a massage therapist simply because she had healing hands. I saw a dietician, an acupuncturist and a yoga guru. None of it helped budge the dizziness, the headaches or my volatile stomach.

I had cut gluten entirely from my diet at this point, which had initially brought some welcome relief from my Crohn's. For about a week I experienced life without severe pain, and without several bathroom trips every hour. Honestly, if hashtags existed back then, for seven lovely days I would have said I was #blessed. But then the honeymoon ended and ordinary proceedings recommenced. I was no longer #blessed.

Because of my erratic stomach, I was on a decent dose of

steroids to alleviate my Crohn's symptoms, which complicated matters. Some of the doctors I saw believed it was possible that the steroids were playing a part in this dizziness, but given the state of my tummy, my gastroenterologist was hesitant to take me off them, *and* he disagreed with the theory that the dizziness was related anyway. As a rule of thumb, the gastroenterologists I saw were reluctant to delve into any part of my health beyond my digestive tract, and the neurologists and ENTs were equally hesitant about dealing with anything other than my dizziness. To me, this seemed perplexing. My Crohn's symptoms and the vertigo were happening simultaneously in *the same body*. It seemed ludicrous that they might not be connected, but I was on my own in that line of thinking.

One Saturday afternoon, I took myself off for a massage in search of 'relaxation', which I knew I desperately needed. It was not a fancy day spa: simply a Chinese massage shop at the bottom of a nearby Westfield that I had been to a few times before. It was a disaster from the moment I laid my head in the designated hole on the bed and attempted to get comfortable.

My heart was palpitating, and lying on my stomach accentuated it. I couldn't escape. My breathing was shallow. The man charged with kneading my muscles noticed my erratic breathing and asked if I was okay. I lied and said I was fine. I wanted to be fine, and I hoped the feeling would pass. It didn't happen. The forty-five minutes were mercilessly long, and I emerged feeling as far from relaxed as I ever had. I could barely pull my jumper back on, and it took a full five minutes for me to find my wallet in my bag and pull out my card to pay.

On the bus home, the palpitations got worse.

What is wrong with you? You just had a massage, you idiot! Why can't you CHILL out???

I got off at Oxford Street and made my way up the stairs. Inside I pulled my pyjamas on, closed the blinds and crawled into bed. I woke up feeling hungover when Nick got home a few hours later. I was so embarrassed by what had happened – what even *had* happened? – that I didn't mention it. I told him I just wanted to catch up on some rest. Inside I went on ruminating.

What makes a person so inept they can't just enjoy a bloody massage?

The truth is, overwrought as I was, there was not a massage therapist in all of Sydney who could have addressed my state of unease.

Denial became much harder to sustain as each day passed, but still I persisted. At the time I was in a very casual book club with a group of girlfriends, and my turn to host a Saturday-afternoon catch-up came around. Considering the state I was in, I could very easily have cancelled or postponed the meeting without it being an issue – after all, those due to attend were my friends – but that did not occur to me. In my rigid mind, cancelling would be tantamount to failure. I couldn't even contemplate that it wouldn't go ahead.

It didn't go ahead. On the Thursday evening before, an acute and painful episode of Crohn's left me in the foetal position, both literally and metaphorically. I could no longer deny that I was losing control. A friend stepped in as the last-minute book club host while I stayed in bed, unable to utter a single word to Nick or Mum, who had flown down to help. I was enveloped in darkness. I wanted to scream as much as I wanted to cry, but silence was all I could muster. This thing – whatever *it* was – was getting on top of me. I could no longer participate in normal life.

Defeated, I called James to explain that I wouldn't be back at work until I got myself better. He was supportive and understanding, as were the vast majority of my colleagues. By that stage I had been in various states of illness for a long time, and the toll it was taking was evident. They wanted me to get better. They were kind.

They're all taking up the slack for you. You're so ungrateful.

I was about to burden my parents too. Nick couldn't be a full-time carer, and I needed full-time care: moving back home was the only option.

After everything they have done for you. After all of the opportunities they gave you. All the love and support and kindness, you are repaying them by becoming a totally dysfunctional and dependent 24-year-old.

But the worst was still to come.

Tell me there is an answer

May 2007

Technically it was after lunch, but that meant nothing in my state. My days were no longer truncated by meals – or routine of any kind. Time was something that existed for other people who were living their lives: for me, not really living, it was meaningless. There was no difference between morning and night, dusk and dawn.

I was in my pyjamas, lying on the sofa that I'd adopted as my refuge, the soft feathers moulded around my lethargic body, when I heard my phone beep. My stomach immediately knotted. I *hated* that sound. Each text alert pierced the veil of denial that had helped me get through each day. It was a reminder that the outside world was real and ongoing, despite my withdrawal from it.

> *Hey G. How are you? Any luck getting rid of the dizziness? Thinking of you. Love Hodge.*

My friend's kind words made me self-conscious; suddenly I was acutely aware of my surroundings. It was as if, by messaging, Hodge could somehow see where I was and what I had become: I was looking at myself through her eyes.

What I saw wasn't good. I was clean but unkempt. Dishevelled. Unmotivated. Pale. Thin. Miserable. Mirrors, hairbrushes, make up and clothes were all foreign by this point, entirely superfluous. A shower and a brush of the teeth were as far as my personal grooming went, and even these were undertaken resentfully.

How was I?

I was effectively unemployed, living back at home with my parents for the first time since I was thirteen. I couldn't walk properly; I could barely eat. I couldn't remember the last day I hadn't spent in my pyjamas on this couch. I couldn't remember occupying a body that didn't feel lank and futile. And I couldn't bring myself to reply to the text because I didn't want to reveal the extent of what I had become.

Hodge's message, like many similar texts in the days and weeks before, was a red flag to the bull that was raging inside me. It made me see myself, and what I saw was terrifying. I wanted to hurl my phone into the wall and watch the shards fly as it smashed, so I would never have to hear from anyone ever again. The rage itself was scary: I'd never experienced anything like it, and now it bubbled perpetually, barely beneath the surface.

'I CAN'T DO THIS!!!' I screamed to no one. I threw my phone, which skated along the tiles but didn't shatter, then slunk off to my bedroom and collapsed on my bed. Adrenaline and fear and fury. I lay on my stomach and buried my head under the pillow, desperate to escape this ferocious rage.

'G,' Mum said softly as she knocked on my door. She had

been in the study when she heard my outburst. 'Darling, can I come in?'

'No! GO AWAY!'

She ignored me, came in and sat on my bed. Her hand was on my back. 'Oh, G.' She sighed. She patted my back and stroked my hair. I cried. She patted. She stroked.

Eventually, she lay down beside me, and even in the dark fog of my fear and loathing, I was so grateful that she did. I was scared, and she made me feel safe. I knew I was unhinged – I'd never felt this untethered, so explosive, so far from being steady.

'I can't do it, Mum,' I lifted the pillow and rolled over to face her.

She wrapped me in her arms as I sobbed. 'I know G,' she said, with love and pity. 'I know.' The rims of her eyes were wet.

'I have no answer,' I said. 'There is no explanation I can give anyone for what's happening. Everyone else can just go about their ordinary lives and I'm here. And there is no answer. There is nothing I can say that makes sense.'

'We'll find an answer, darling. I know this is awful but we will get you better.'

'That's not true, Mum. How can it be?'

'You will not always feel like this. I know you won't.'

I didn't believe her.

Eventually I stopped crying and Mum got up, but I couldn't. The rage had wiped me out. Mum brought in tea and tried to coax me into coming out and eating something, but I wouldn't. I stayed in bed for the rest of the day. Even the living room was too much to face, and sitting up for dinner was beyond me. Hiding in bed nursing the hangover from my fiery, fear-laden outburst was all I could manage.

Contemplating the extent to which my physical health and the practicalities of my life had disintegrated hurt, and saying it out loud made it worse. Deep down, I feared that there was no answer to this nightmare because it was all in my head. I didn't worry that I was in the grips of mental illness; I worried that I was quite simply insane. That I was imagining the dizziness. The fact I could no longer hold myself together made me more certain – and frightened – that I was going mad.

The only way I could keep going was to not think about the big picture. I could get through each day if I only focused on what was in front of me in that moment. It meant actively ignoring the real world, including many attempts at contact from friends.

To escape reality, I became weirdly, and wholly, obsessed with watching *Big Brother* and sport, two forms of entertainment I had never previously enjoyed. But both were on TV often, and I could invest myself sufficiently in the contestants and players to distract myself from having to think too deeply about my life. Trashy TV was numbing, and following the schedule of various rugby league teams, inexplicably, provided me with refuge (a sentence that is as alien to me now as it was before the vertigo).

Using a combination of carer's leave and long-service leave, Mum had been able to take on the thankless task of being my carer, and my parents and I had quickly fallen into roles. Mum was the tireless patient advocate; I was the miserable, moody invalid; and Dad was the peacemaker, responsible for bringing levity to the wholly unfunny crisis playing out in his living room. He would regularly bring home stand-up comedy DVDs – anything to get a laugh. He religiously watched *Big Brother* with me, and even managed to appear interested.

Mum was dogged in her pursuit of an answer to my woes: finding a solution occupied her day and night. She researched my symptoms, booked appointments, found new treatments, rang doctors, bought or borrowed every health-related book she could get her hands on, managed my moods, caught my wrath far too often and did everything she could to ensure I wouldn't need to spend the rest of my life on her couch.

I started seeing a new GP, ENT specialist and gastroenterologist in the local area, and visits to an acupuncturist who came well recommended were added to my roster of appointments. Mum organised for a psychologist to come to see me once a week at home because I was so flat.

There was no obvious improvement in my physical symptoms, and my Crohn's continued to flare up. I was admitted to the Lismore base hospital twice because of my intractable stomach. The vertigo persisted, and feeling weak, dizzy and nauseous was my new normal – to the extent that I couldn't actually remember ever having felt any different. The trouble with my multiple health-issues continued: none of the medical practitioners I was seeing was willing to delve beyond their area of expertise, so it was up to us to try to piece it all together.

Mum cast the net wide for solutions, working to the theory that if we tried absolutely everything, surely *something* would eventually help. I tried every manner of natural therapy available, while also accessing every mainstream health service we could find.

The only reason I ever left the house was to attend appointments, which happened a few times each week. Initially I didn't mind these outings, and the hope that came from seeing someone new who might be able to help, but a few weeks in, the gloss had well and truly worn off.

I would begrudgingly get dressed into something other than my pyjamas, brush my hair and use a slick of tinted moisturiser to hide my pallor. I'd slowly make my way to the car with Mum, tentative about being outside, and inevitably sulk for the duration of the trip.

Aside from the energy these outings required, they had become a real source of tension between Mum and me.

'G, you don't need to pretend to be feeling better than you are,' she said one afternoon before she even turned on the ignition.

'I'm not!' I replied indignantly. 'Why would I do that?'

'I see you, G. I see the state you are in and you are not letting that on to these doctors. You sit down and you smile and you speak matter-of-factly and they think you're fine.'

'What do you want me to do? Lie down on the floor and cry? Scream?'

'No. I just want you to be honest about how this is impacting you,' she said, then started the car.

'I am! Of course I'm being honest.'

We didn't speak for the ten-minute drive into town. I knew she had a point. I wasn't revealing the true extent of the problem, but I didn't know how to. The thought of letting down my guard to a medical professional terrified me. As a result, I drove Mum absolutely batty. We had a version of this argument virtually every time we ventured outside.

Soon I dreaded all appointments, not only because I resented having to leave the sofa and hated the fight they would set off, but because the loss of hope was demoralising. Every time I came away deflated, crushed and angry. What was the point in venturing out to see another person so that they could tell me they didn't know what was wrong?

Still, I did as I was told.

We – and I say 'we' because Mum and Dad joined in – tried a variety of different diets in an attempt to alleviate my symptoms. We went gluten-free, sugar-free and dairy-free, but salicylate-free (aka taste-free) was, without question, the real low point. Mum emptied the pantry and bathroom cupboards of all products containing certain preservatives and replaced them with salicylate-free shampoo, conditioner, toothpaste, dishwashing detergent and every other household item she could find. It's laughable now, but there was no humour the night we sat down to gluten-free pasta with what was generously described as 'salicylate-free bolognese sauce', which consisted of onion dry fried with super-lean mince. The dinner looked – and tasted – as miserable as I felt.

An informal family conscription program had come into effect shortly after I moved back home, whereby various members of my family were enlisted to visit for weekends to distract me from myself and take some of the pressure off Mum and Dad. My aunties, my grandpa, my sister, my brother-in-law and my brother were all roped in, and while their company was always welcome, it was hard for me to ignore that their visits were only necessitated by my current state. I felt like a helpless animal in a zoo.

But they all tried.

'Mum, where I am supposed to hold this?' my younger brother, Chris, called out to Mum one evening before dinner, a slightly pained look on his face.

'Just below her knee, and you need to hold it about ten centimetres away,' Mum said, walking over to us.

It was a Friday evening and I was sitting up on the couch with my legs out in front of me while my brother, who had come home from Brisbane for the weekend, held what looked like a lit cigar over my skin.

As younger kids, Chris and I had fought quite a bit: to me he was a typically annoying younger sibling, and to him I was an equally irritating older sister. He was as consistent at antagonising me – from bouncing balls on the door of my bedroom to mimicking me – as I was in reacting. But as we got older, Chris and I grew out of the shared irritation, and by the time we both finished school we'd become close.

Even so, him delivering 'health care' to me was new terrain. He was attempting to administer moxibustion, a traditional Chinese medicine therapy recommended by my acupuncturist. It involves burning dried, musty-smelling mugwort over particular points on the body. I wasn't expecting much from the therapy; it was just something to do – *anything* was better than nothing. Chris was certainly no expert; in fact he'd never heard of the treatment until Mum roped him in ten minutes earlier. Still, he'd agreed and was now sitting beside me with a solemn, monk-like expression, dutifully hovering the stick above my shin for the requisite ninety seconds … that is, until our eyes finally met, and we both roared laughing.

It was a rare – and welcome – relief.

I haven't ever asked my relatives to recount their own experiences of visiting at this time, but I know this type of laughter was unusual. Their visits were rarely enjoyable. Fodder for conversation was limited, given pretty much anything involving the future was a no-go zone. Everyone was dancing on eggshells trying not to antagonise me. Because I was easily goaded, as Chris discovered the next day. His visit had coincided with my latest diet change, which consisted of liquid smoothies specially designed for Crohn's sufferers. In a bid to get my irritable stomach under control, for a few days at a time I would give up real food and instead consume these foul-tasting medical poppers. Naturally, this did nothing for my already-hostile mood.

No one else could join me on this particular diet – not that I could imagine them ever wanting to – so during these times, everyone in the house concealed their consumption of food to avoid confronting me with it. The fact I was spending a lot of time in my room made this relatively easy, but unfortunately one Saturday afternoon I stepped out at the wrong time.

I was in a state of gloom, walking towards the kitchen from my room to get a glass of water, when I caught Chris putting the finishing touches on a sourdough sandwich that I could see was loaded with avocado, chicken, aioli and tomato. The sight and smell of real food laden with flavour – with gluten, dairy *and* salicylates – was more than I could bear. Hearing my movement, Chris looked up and his face fell with guilt.

I turned back around, returned to my room, slammed the door and cried. Again. (During this time I more than made up for the fact that Mum and Dad, having sent their kids to boarding schools, hadn't really endured moody teenagers at home.)

Chris knocked and came in, looking sheepish.

'I'm sorry, G. I thought you were asleep.'

I was embarrassed and couldn't speak.

'G, I'm so sorry,' he said, with a pained expression. 'I feel terrible.'

'You're allowed to eat,' I eventually replied. 'Of course you're allowed to eat. I just wish I could eat too.'

'So do I! Honestly, G, I don't know how you're handling this.'

'Not very well is the answer.'

'It sucks. We all wish we could make it better. If I could take it away from you I would.'

'I know that.'

There was an awkward pause as he hovered in the doorway. 'Time for more burning sticks?' he asked.

I laughed, wiping my face. 'Why not? Maybe *moxibustion* is what I really need.'

~

Throughout those months, self-pity and envy drenched my thoughts. No one else – at least no one I could see – was on this hellish boat ride. No one else was confined to their childhood home, unable to participate in life, with no end in sight. I could see how desperately those closest to me wanted to provide a dock so I could disembark my nightmare and resume ordinary life, but no one could give that to me.

One afternoon, Mum came into my bedroom with her usual offer of a cup of tea. When I declined, she paused for a moment, then sat down on the corner of my bed. I noticed she was holding some printed sheets of A4 paper.

'G, I've been doing some research and I think we have to think about anxiety as a factor in what you're experiencing.'

I couldn't believe it. We'd been over this before.

'Mum, I haven't felt well for months. Of course I'm anxious! Anyone in this position would be.' I practically spat the words at her.

'You don't have to get angry at me, G. I'm trying to help.'

'Well, I *am* angry at you. You come in here and tell me that my problem might be *anxiety*? Yes, I am bloody anxious, and

I will be until someone can tell me why I've got this goddamn vertigo and how to make it go away.'

Mum looked down, silent. I had pushed too far. I didn't know whether she was going to yell or cry; I suspect she wanted to do both.

She did neither.

'Read this checklist. That's all I'm asking,' she said, placing the papers on my bed. 'You tick every box.' She walked out.

I refused to look at them. Instead I grabbed my phone and shot a message off to Nick.

> Just had a fight with Mum :-(She thinks the vertigo is caused by anxiety. Can you believe that? Of course I'm anxious now! There's a checklist apparently and I tick every box.

Oh darling, don't fight with Jan. She is trying to help. What is the checklist?

> I don't care! I'm not even looking at it.

Georgie …

> Ok, I read the checklist and I tick some boxes but that's obvious ... I'm dizzy and unwell so I've become anxious. I just need someone to fix this bloody vertigo and then the rest will go away.

> I've got to go but will call tonight. Be nice to Jan.

I really should have been, and not just because Nick said so. Pouring every ounce of love, time and energy she had into helping me wasn't without its challenges for my mum. Her mental health suffered. How could it not? She had been, rightly, worried for months before this point, and now I was crumbling before her eyes. And so was she. She lost weight, became depressed and struggled almost as much as I did, which really upped the ante for Dad. Soon enough he was watching his wife *and* one of his daughters simultaneously fall apart, and it was up to him to somehow help us both.

I woke up early one quiet Saturday morning and stayed hidden in my room, willing the time away, until after 8am. Why couldn't time just disappear altogether? When I came out, Dad was sitting up at the kitchen bench with the weekend paper spread out, and toast and tea.

'Good morning!' he said cheerfully. 'What can I get you to eat?'

'Nothing. I'm not hungry,' I said.

The house felt strangely still.

'Where's Mum?'

There was a pause. 'She's gone over to Yamba to see Pa and Sal,' Dad said.

A torrent of sadness and fear struck me. She'd fled me to be with her dad and sister.

'Does she want to run away …?' My voice broke before I got the whole question out.

It was understandable that Mum might need some time to herself, and yet the idea was strangely wounding. I didn't want her to be trapped caring for me, but I didn't want her to need a break from me either. I couldn't stand the thought that meeting my myriad needs had felled her. I needed her to be able to cope.

'Can she not cope with me anymore?' I asked Dad as I burst into tears and curled into the couch.

'Hey, G. No, not at all. She's just exhausted and we thought it would be good for her to have the weekend in Yamba.'

'To get away from me? Because I'm so awful?'

'No, not because you're awful! You're not awful, G. You're having a rough time, and Mum is too.'

Dad sat beside me on the couch as I sobbed, adopting the position that had become Mum's default over the past month. I remember thinking it was inexplicable that I hadn't run out of tears or fear or anger yet. Surely, there had to be a limit? There wasn't. Sobbing for several hours one day didn't preclude from me doing it again the next day. And the next. Unfurling my fear and succumbing to white rage in primal explosions didn't stop me from doing that again either. Each day presented a new, bottomless pit. There was no end to my capacity for sadness, for fear, for anger.

I struggled to snap out of it and I wondered how long it would take before Dad needed to run away from me too. How many times can a parent sit comforting their inconsolable adult child without breaking? Mum had long exceeded the limit. I didn't want to ruin her life, but I couldn't live without her.

The days crept by and my desperation became less tolerable. For every bit of hope I had pinned on a certain doctor or particular treatment, there was a bigger fear that they wouldn't have the answer or their treatment wouldn't work. My fear grew, and so did my anger, simmering below the surface of my skin, sporadically manifesting itself in outbursts of rage. I was so loved, but the more that people wanted to help, the lonelier I felt.

Nick was a rare bright speck in a bleak period. At the time he was juggling studying full-time for his medical degree with a rugby career: he had been playing first-grade rugby for a team in Sydney virtually since we'd met, and he'd been picked to participate in a trial of a new professional national competition. He'd been selected for the ACT-based team, which meant he was commuting between Sydney and Canberra several times a week. (The explanation for how Nick managed to juggle these commitments lies in the fact he is a human Energiser Bunny: he never stops.)

His long and regular commute actually lent itself well to the strange circumstances of our relationship, as did the fact we had mastered the art of long phone calls during our first year together. Depending on my mental state, which was usually teetering precariously between denial and despair, Nick would distract me with stories from his day and his plans for us – big and small – that I didn't believe would ever eventuate.

There were joyless conversations too. Plenty of them. Sometimes Nick would just listen to me cry; there were days, many days, when tears were the only thing I could offer. On days like these, there were no words that could help, but by being on the other end of the phone – staying there through tears and silence – he offered me a lifeline.

Every few weeks on a Saturday afternoon, Nick's rugby matches were televised, which meant I could watch him play. Each time, regardless of the score or his performance, my heart would burst with a mixture of pride and love, not because of his sporting prowess but because of what I knew was happening behind the scenes. Out of loyalty to me and his general preference for discretion, no one around him knew the full extent of my troubles. No one really knew the emotional burden he was carrying. There was no sign of him suffering: somehow he was able to persevere with his degree, his rugby and his ailing girlfriend without dropping a single ball. Quite literally.

Nick's phone calls and visits punctured the monotony, but before any of his visits to Lismore my mood would darken. The idea of seeing him, and him seeing me in this state, sickened me. Not because of vanity, though that played a minor part, but because instead of enjoying our new little flat together, we were living apart. And I was falling apart. The contrast between us could not have been more stark. He was undertaking a medical degree and being paid to play sport, while a good day for me was having a shower and getting out of my pyjamas. Why would he want to be part of that?

I would wrap myself in a tight ball of angst before he arrived, and then, slowly, I would unravel during his visit. Just having him close made me feel better. He made me laugh. He made me feel happy and reminded me of the life I was missing. It made me want to be better, but it also compounded my anguish because I couldn't leave with him and return to our normal life.

At the end of June, Nick and I were contacted by our real estate agent. The landlord was terminating our lease early, and we had two weeks to move out. Physically I was in no state to pack up a suitcase let alone an apartment, so Dad flew down to Sydney and helped Nick to move us out. Some of my relatives offered us their garages for storage, which we gratefully accepted.

Even though at that point it was unimaginable that I would ever be well enough to live anywhere except my parents' sofa, being forced to move out was gutting. Nick was spending so much time in Canberra that it wasn't a disaster for him, but for me, the flat was the last physical proof of my life in Sydney, and giving it up added another layer to the displacement I felt.

My beacon of hope was the Guru. Mum had issued a challenge to our extended family and friends, and their families and friends, asking everyone to utilise every contact they had to see if someone could get in touch with the Guru. To get on a cancellation list, to have another name suggested, to have some mysterious and magical explanation provided. Honestly, we just wanted something. My extended family is big and determined, but the Guru eluded their best efforts. The closest we got was a senior specialist at the same hospital, a friend of my mum's cousin, who stalked the Guru's rooms, but even he couldn't get inside.

We would have to wait – and I wish I could say I was patient about it. After every failed treatment, inconclusive test or fruitless consultation, and there were many, I'd cry, become frustrated, get mad and lose hope. But eventually, hours or sometimes days later, I'd pull myself together and remember my appointment with the Guru. If there was an answer to my spinning head, I was certain the Guru had it. I just had to, somehow, get through to my appointment in September.

The lowest ebb

August 2007

'Darling, please, let me help you home. *Please* ... I will carry you. Let's just get you inside.'

It was pitch-black, cold and I was lying in a ditch beside the road at the end of my parents' street. I could hear Nick's voice, but his words weren't registering over my own deafening thoughts.

WHEN WILL THIS END???
IT WAS MEANT TO BE A SHORT WALK! THE KIND OF THING NORMAL PEOPLE DO ALL THE TIME!
WHAT THE HELL IS WRONG WITH YOU???

It was a winter evening, the night before Nick was due to fly back to Sydney. We had set out with the modest objective of walking to the end of the street for some fresh air. It had been more than three months since I'd left Sydney, and to say I had cabin fever was an understatement.

Because of this, in line with her many and varied attempts to prop me up, Mum had been making me walk to the end of their street and back with her once a day, a task I found thoroughly depressing. Outside, on the street where I rode my bike as a child, where I walked with my sister to primary school, where we all got swooped by magpies, there was no hiding from what had become of me. I was a young woman barely able to walk three hundred metres. The blinding daylight skewered the denial I was able to maintain inside with the curtains drawn, under the comfort of the doona on my bed or the blanket on the sofa. Getting outside made shutting out the world impossible, so I avoided it as much as I could. Which is why I surprised myself when I agreed to Nick's suggestion that we go for a short walk after dinner.

Yes! I thought. *Like normal people do! Like we used to!*

I'd been doing well, managing the walk relatively easily, until a dreaded vertigo attack swooped at the very end of the street and knocked me off balance. I bent over and leaned on Nick before falling to my knees and lying down with my eyes clenched shut.

I didn't want to go home. I didn't want to move. I just wanted it all to stop. I lay on the damp grass and refused to budge. I'd had enough. I felt beaten and devoid of hope and all I wanted, all I desperately wanted, was to go to sleep and wake up when this was all over.

For the longest time I just lay there. I didn't cry or yell or speak. I couldn't. I couldn't bring myself to look Nick in the eye because I knew I was losing it. I knew things had been bad, but this was worse still. How could I mentally manoeuvre around the fact that I was lying motionless in a ditch in the dead of winter, ignoring the desperate and sensible pleas of the person I loved? I was mortified it had come to this.

Because we didn't have a phone with us, Nick couldn't call for help and he didn't want to leave me there alone. So he kneeled beside me, stroked my face and pleaded with me to let him help me home. His voice was so sad and scared, which compounded the cacophony raging inside my head. In that moment I hated myself and what was happening more viscerally than I had ever hated anything before. The misery I was inflicting was as excruciating as the despair I couldn't escape.

He doesn't deserve this. He deserves happiness. He deserves a girlfriend who can function as a regular member of society: he does not need a mentally unstable, physically unwell shell of a woman to drag him down. You need to set him free. You don't deserve him and he certainly doesn't deserve you.

Eventually, thirty minutes later, I relented and let Nick help me up and take me home, but I still couldn't speak or look at him. I was so embarrassed. I dissolved into tears as soon as we got inside and went straight to bed. I don't remember exactly what happened next, but I remember how ashamed I felt. I remember the anguish in Nick's eyes, and it was exquisitely painful to realise how much I was making him hurt.

It was August; I could no longer pretend that I was mentally okay. The distinction I had angrily clung to about my mental distress relating exclusively to my physical illness seemed less viable. When I had arrived in Lismore in May it was my physical symptoms, my spinning head and calamitous stomach, that I was desperate to quell. Early on it had felt like I was losing my mind because I had lost my body, but several months on I was beginning to wonder if it might have been the other way around. Was I losing my body because I had lost my mind? I didn't know, but I could no longer muster the energy to deny that, psychologically, I was compromised.

Aside from confirming that I needed help, this incident in the ditch crystallised a sickening thought that had been bothering me. Nick didn't need this. He had a happy life ahead of him and he didn't need to be weighed down by me. It broke my heart to contemplate, but it was easier than imagining him being subject to me for the rest of his life. We had fallen in love, madly so, but I was faulty. An ill-manufactured good. My mind still contained enough legal knowledge for me to know what came next: at the time of purchase my flaws were not known, so Nick was entitled to return me. It required action, as I explained to him when we next spoke on the phone.

'You will be better off without me,' I told him. 'You don't need this.'

He paused before replying. 'Are you serious? Why would you even say that?' The hurt was audible.

'Think about it. I am broken. I can't imagine that I am ever going to be well enough to be normal ever again, and you don't need that. You deserve something better and, frankly, anyone else would be better than me right now. You have the world at your feet. I'm a sinking ship and you don't need to go down with me.'

'That is not true. You will get better.'

We had versions of the same conversation for a week. I said he needed to be set free, that I had found at least one solution to all the problems my illness was creating. He said I wasn't thinking straight, that this was a terrible 'solution' to a temporary problem.

During these circular, draining conversations, I came perilously close to convincing Nick we should go our separate ways, and I am still, ten years on, grateful that he overruled me. He wasn't leaving, he said, even if it was what I thought I wanted. I would get better, he insisted. And while I was certain he was wrong, I didn't have it in me to fight him on it.

I didn't have it in me to fight anything, really, because by now I was truly depressed, and had been for some time. My sessions with the psychologist who had been visiting me at home were getting worse and worse. When I'd begun seeing her, we'd been able to strategise different methods for managing my emotions, coping day to day and responding to communication. Now I was often unable to speak. I was utterly inconsolable, and I cried in those sessions, in those weeks, like I have never cried before. I cried outside the sessions too. Nothing else I had – or have since – experienced comes close to the helplessness and hopelessness that swallowed me up towards the end of my confinement.

For months it had felt like things couldn't possibly get any worse, and yet somehow things had got worse. The only conclusion I could reach was that this whole thing was in my head. That the vertigo and dizziness weren't real, that I was somehow imagining it because I couldn't cope with life like everyone else could.

The enormity of that fear – that I had veered from sanity – is traumatic, even now, to confront. I was the furthest I had ever been from reality and I very seriously doubted that I was ever going to feel any differently.

Mum kept working in the background to find help wherever and however she could. We'd given up on the diets, with the exception of eating gluten-free, and the list of medical professionals I'd seen was now pages long, but Mum persisted.

Four months after I'd first returned to Lismore, finally, something changed. An opportunity to consult with a Dr Wagner, a seventy-year-old physician on the cusp of retirement, presented itself. Unbeknown to me, word of my predicament had spread through the Lismore medical fraternity, and this gentleman had offered to see me.

Mum and I went through the motions of getting ready for an appointment. I dreaded having somewhere to be and needing to exit the house, so I did my best impression of a recalcitrant toddler.

Mum came to my room to nudge me along. 'G, we'll need to leave in half an hour. Would you like to have a shower?'

'No.'

'Put some clothes on?'

'Not really. I like my pyjamas.'

'Come on, G.'

She left me alone for ten minutes before coming back, hoping I'd at least taken a step towards getting ready. I hadn't.

'G?' she said, properly exasperated.

'What? I don't want to get dressed.'

'We are leaving here in fifteen minutes and if you aren't dressed you can come in your pyjamas. You still have time for a shower.'

She was cross and I was stubborn, but five minutes before I knew we had to leave, I begrudgingly got out of bed and pulled on a pair of jeans and a jumper. I really didn't want to go to the appointment, but my desire not to disappoint Mum was stronger. Beneath my stubbornness, I knew how weary she had grown of our battles.

I sat in silence in the passenger seat as we drove into town. Upon our arrival at Dr Wagner's rooms across the road from the base hospital, I felt certain that nothing would come from the appointment. By this point it seemed clear that no new doctor, with the possible exception of the Guru, could provide any insight. (My appointment with the Guru was crawling closer but it wasn't close enough.)

Mum and I took seats across from Dr Wagner's as he went through reams and reams of paper – blood test results, medical reports, CT scans, MRI results, countless referral letters. He read, asked the occasional question and looked me in the eye each time I answered. After ten minutes, he closed the folder, laid his hands together on the top of his desk and appeared to gather his thoughts before speaking.

'Georgie, I am so sorry for what you are going through,' he said, looking right into my eyes. 'It is just awful.'

His compassion threw me, and initially I thought I must have misheard him. As it registered that he had actually said the words I thought I'd heard him say, I blinked back tears. It was such a simple thing to say, but it wasn't a sentiment any other medical professional had offered. In an instant I felt understood and validated. It *had* been awful. I was going through *'something'*. The armour I was so accustomed to wearing in these consultations dropped.

'What you are going through is real,' he said. 'In my experience as a physician who has practised for more than thirty years, I have come to learn that stress has a very real impact on the body. Whenever I see a patient who has a condition that is flaring up without any obvious physical cause, or has unexplained physical symptoms, stress is always the reason.'

He explained that whether stress had caused my vertigo in the first place was less important now than dealing with the psychological distress caused by the past few months.

'Whatever else is happening, it is clear that you are now in a bad way, which anybody in this situation would be, and we need to consider how we can address what you are experiencing.'

I listened, and I actually heard him. I didn't get my back

up as I had in the past. I didn't even contemplate saying, *Of course I am bloody stressed. I haven't been able to live properly for four months!* I didn't need to battle to be heard or understood. Relief flooded my mind. He was right. I knew he was right. There wasn't an elaborate or mysterious medical explanation for what was happening to me but there was *something* we could do.

He recommended I see a psychiatrist as soon as possible with a view to being assessed and admitted to an in-patient facility. Before we were even back in the car, an appointment with a shrink had been arranged for the next day, and I had an inkling that change was coming.

The next morning, I fronted up and answered honestly when I was assessed by a warm and congenial female psychiatrist. It was evident that I was clinically depressed and suffering from chronic anxiety, so she tabled some medication and a stint in rehab as the best course of action. I swallowed my pride and agreed.

Some phone calls were made and a private psychiatric facility on the Gold Coast was recommended as the preferred option. Once referrals were written, phone calls were made and health insurance was confirmed, I was offered a two-week stint, starting the following week. But, as was the universe's wont, my place in rehab coincided with my long-awaited appointment with the Guru, and roughly one thousand kilometres of Australian countryside separated the two. I knew I needed rehab, but I was unwilling to forgo my appointment. Anxiety and depression aside, if there was a medical explanation for my vertigo, I was sure the Guru would have it.

Mum was as adamant that I should take up the spot in rehab immediately as I was that I had to see the Guru first. Not for the first time in those months, Dad arrived home from work to find

Mum and me in the middle of an almighty row.

How could she not understand why I couldn't give up my long-awaited spot with the Guru?!

How could I not understand why I need to go to rehab to get better?!

We were both distraught, wearied from our months in our joint battle for my health, and Dad, also wearied, was caught in the middle. There were tears, more doors slammed and angry accusations screamed across the various rooms of our family home. Dad ferried himself between us and somehow negotiated a solution: if it was possible to move my rehab start date by one week, I could see the Guru before I went.

The next morning it was arranged: Dad and I would fly to Sydney on Thursday evening to make the Friday-morning appointment, and I would start rehab the following week. Mum, quite understandably, needed a break, and she didn't have it in her to accompany me to Sydney – which, in hindsight, was a blessing.

By this point I had flown back to Sydney twice in the past month to see two different neurologists. The visits were brief but taxing. Everything, from getting out the door in Lismore, to being in public at the airports and on the plane, getting to the waiting rooms, waiting for my turn to be scanned or prodded or questioned, was exhausting. Returning to Sydney was confronting too. I felt misplaced. I wasn't, technically, a resident anymore and I could barely handle the pace of it for a day. But how could I *not* be a resident? I wasn't willing to let go of my life there.

I survived each of these trips to the city because of my hope that these neurologists would have an answer. On this trip, the stakes seemed even higher, but my sense of hope was higher still. *Finally* I would meet the expert I had patiently been waiting months and months to see, the man who could deliver the definitive diagnosis on my vertigo.

The night before the appointment, Dad and I stayed alone in the apartment of some family friends. The Guru's rooms were on the other side of Sydney, so we woke early to ensure we wouldn't be late. After crossing the city in our hire car and finding a parking spot, we still had time to grab a quick breakfast from a cafe around the corner. Butterflies swarmed in my stomach as I downed my coffee: I couldn't quite believe this day was here.

After checking into reception and being asked to pay the eye-watering $500 consultation fee up front, we sat and waited. And waited. An hour and a half passed before the Guru ushered us in.

'Georgina,' the wiry man quickly called out, then disappeared back to wherever he had come from.

Dad and I stood up and followed.

'I'm Michael, Georgie's father,' Dad said by way of explanation as we stood inside his room.

'Sit,' the Guru said, with apparent disinterest. He flipped through a wad of papers, presumably the various referrals, test results and medical records I had needed to provide.

I wondered what he was searching for. 'What are—'

'*Shhh*,' he said.

After a few minutes he raised his eyebrows.

'Well, I've got to say, it is confusing that some of your doctors are in Lismore and others are in Sydney,' he said. 'Why is that?'

'I had to move home a few months ago because I've been unwell and couldn't really look after myself ...' I started.

He looked up with a wry grin. 'Ah! I see, so you two have been meeting somewhere in the middle for romantic trysts?'

I nearly choked. 'He's my father,' I said.

'Georgie and I travelled to Sydney together from our home in Lismore for this appointment,' Dad said, the colour draining from his face.

The doctor laughed it off without any sign of embarrassment. Any hope I had harboured of a miraculous diagnosis was rapidly diminishing.

'Now, Georgie, I'm just going to say this. From looking at you, it is quite obvious that you are what I'd call a "cappuccino" kind of girl,' he said peering over his glasses at me.

I must have looked confused, because he continued.

'Let's be honest, you would quite like a leisurely life. That's probably what you are best suited to, isn't it?'

That was the sum total of the medical advice he offered. Having looked at me for less than ten minutes, during which time he mistook my dad for my long-distance love interest and asked not a single question about my symptoms or history, he concluded I was a princess with a weak constitution. A 'cappuccino girl'.

To this day it takes my breath away to relive that appointment. Dad and I were nothing short of shell-shocked as we made our way back to the car. We barely spoke. I had encountered some less than impressive doctors in my time, but no one came close to being as disdainful as that man was. Tears stung my eyes as we drove back to the airport.

It finally sank in what would happen next. I would be going to a psychiatric hospital. The thought was confronting, but somehow it made me feel better. Without knowing there was something else coming up, something that could fix me, I'm not sure how I would have recovered from the crushing disappointment of that meeting. Even rehab had to be better than this.

Part Two
Broken

I gotta go to rehab

September 2007

'Dad, pull over,' I whispered. 'I need to get out.'

'Okay, try to just breathe. I'll pull over as soon as I can.'

I was nauseous and sweaty and felt like I was suffocating. The back seat of my parents' car had never felt so small, and I pulled at a loose thread in the seat's upholstery to distract myself from the rising panic.

This wasn't the first time I'd asked Dad to stop. We had survived the windy road between Lismore and Bangalow; the familiar lush landscape had passed in a blur, but once we hit the highway the truth had hit me. Toxic adrenaline began pumping through my veins and I felt like I was going to combust. Twice already Dad had pulled into a shoulder beside the highway so I could escape. Twice, I'd attempted to throw up and ended up dry-retching so much that I expected to dislodge an internal organ.

Being driven to a psychiatric hospital by my parents wasn't an experience I'd ever expected to have. Rehab was all the rage in 2007, with a slew of 'it' girls like Lindsay Lohan, Britney Spears and Nicole Ritchie checking in to various facilities amid blazes of publicity, but their admissions variously involved illicit substances, misdemeanours and public meltdowns. I had never taken a puff of a cigarette (true story) and was straighter than an arrow: I was your white-bread, run-of-the-mill, boring, good girl. I'd worked hard, turned up to class, handed in assignments on time, didn't cram for exams, applied for jobs and diligently attended work. Even the *idea* of deviating from the rails was alien to me, and yet there I was, being driven to a private psychiatric hospital in Queensland.

At the risk of sounding dramatic, I didn't expect to survive the car trip. Fight or flight had set in and my body wanted both, simultaneously.

Eventually, after five ghastly roadside stops, we reached our destination and pulled into the carpark of a small hospital tucked a kilometre or so from the beach in the Gold Coast hinterland.

'Right!' Mum gallantly attempted enthusiasm as Dad navigated the car into an empty spot right out the front of the building that was to be my new temporary home. 'At least the car trip is over!'

Once the car was stationary I no longer wanted to escape. Surveying the blond-brick building ahead, plain and tired and sad, made me want to stay in the car. Forever.

Sensing my paralysis, Dad opened my door.

'You okay …?' he asked, his voice carrying the warmth that had marked my life as his child. The rims of his eyes were wet, a sight that wrenched. I wasn't okay and I really didn't want to move, but I knew I needed to. I had dug in enough.

Dad squeezed my shoulders after I stepped out of the car. Mum walked around to where I stood and wrapped her arms around me while Dad retrieved my small suitcase from the boot. Affection expressed what words couldn't.

'Well,' Mum said as the three of us walked the ten metres to the entrance. We rang the bell, and as the wide white doors were buzzed open, my heart sank further.

There was no mistaking it. I was entering a locked institution, and if the outside had looked sad, it was positively resort-like compared to this waiting room. The reception staff were behind glass, the lino floor might have once been white but was now yellowing, and the grey plastic chairs were filled with patients, many of whom were visibly dissembling, ready to be checked in. We were told to take a seat and wait for my name to be called.

We sat down and scanned the room. It goes without saying that rehab is hardly a destination many aspire to visit, and the heartache was palpable. I was one of many very lost and seriously unwell souls in that room. I tried to guess who was being admitted and who was playing the support role and wondered which was worse. Neither position looked particularly appealing.

As each minute passed, my misgivings about what even a night in this place would be like escalated. The facility admitted patients into one of two wards, one for mood disorders and one for substance abuse, so I mentally assigned my new housemates into those categories. Despite the distinctions in the physical demeanours of the men and women around me, there was one common characteristic: the flicker of fear in the eyes. Whether they were being admitted themselves, or they were admitting a loved one, *everyone* was scared.

Eventually my name was called and we were taken into a small antechamber off the waiting room.

'Georgina, do you understand why you are being admitted today?' the business-like admissions manager asked, not even making eye contact as she peered through the paperwork.

I believe it's because I have become a complete basket case who can no longer exist or function as an independent adult.

While her head stayed perfectly still, her eyes rose sharply to meet mine.

'Yes. I haven't been very well.'

'Georgina, do you understand that this is a hospital and as an admitted patient you are required to follow the rules as outlined in this booklet?'

A hospital? That facade out the front is totally misleading, I fully thought this was a resort!

'Yes.'

'Do you understand that there is to be no alcohol, no drugs and no medication kept in your room?'

'Yes.'

'You may have your phone but it cannot be taken outside of your room and it must be kept on silent at all times.'

The officious admissions manager took me through a mountain of paperwork, and all the logistics and rigid conditions of my stay, before the contents of my bag were examined piece by piece and my various medications were logged.

Each step of becoming an in-patient in this complex chipped away at the pretence I'd been trying to maintain: that this wasn't really happening. Being led down a hallway to the room that would be mine for the next few weeks was the point at which I was forced to surrender. This *was* happening.

The nurse slowed down to signal we had reached my room. As we entered, I saw three women huddled together. It was clear they were related – three versions of the same lean physique – though one was evidently older than the other two.

The distress on the faces of the two younger women looked familiar. It matched Mum and Dad's.

'Georgie, this is Sue,' the nurse said, pointing to the older woman. 'You'll be sharing this room for your stay.'

Sue and I made eye contact and nodded nervously before she continued out our door and down the hall to say goodbye to her visitors.

Ours looked like any other two-bed hospital room, with lino floors, a shared bathroom and curtain partitions to separate the beds. There were two small sets of drawers, two chairs and two single beds. The curtains were faded and the paint was chipped, but at least it didn't look like a jail cell.

Sue had claimed the bed closest to the door, which meant I got the window bed. Mum started to help unpack my things and Dad looked out over the bushland beside the property. I put things away slowly, knowing that once that task was done my parents would leave.

Walking back to the hospital foyer to say our goodbyes felt painfully reminiscent of my first day at boarding school. I was scared of what their leaving might trigger. Here I didn't have my sister to run to. I was on my own.

'I love you, darling,' Mum said as she squeezed my bony frame.
'I love you too.'
'G, you take care, okay?' Dad said. 'You promise?'
'I promise.'
'We're coming to get you as soon as you feel better, okay?'
'Okay.'

The past few days had been fraught with panic about being here, about this moment, about being left alone in this foreign place, but as I walked back to my room I felt strange.

Who finds relief in a psychiatric facility? I wondered. Almost immediately, I answered the question for myself: *A person who needs it. A person like me.*

My roommate Sue was lying on her bed when I returned to the room.

'Soooo ...' I said as I caught her eyes.

We both sort of laughed in acknowledgement of this unusual situation: two total strangers brought together only by the fact we were concurrently suffering through the worst days of our lives. And we were sharing a room for the ride.

'They were my daughters,' Sue explained when I asked about the two women I'd seen her with earlier. 'I feel sick because they have already been through so much and now they have to go through this too.'

'I feel the same about my parents.'

We spent an hour traversing the intimate terrain of what had led us each here. Given where we were, there was no point pretending that either one of us was coping. The year before, Sue had been diagnosed with breast cancer and the chemo and treatment had knocked her around badly. Like me, in becoming accustomed to diminished physical health, she had grown depressed and anxious. Her physical and psychological symptoms had become so interlinked that it was hard to know where one stopped and the other started.

Our lives were very different, and yet we had landed in the same place, in the same room, at the same time. The comfort in meeting a person who understood, in real time, the grief and fear associated with losing your grip on ordinary life, was immense. I wouldn't wish the experience of being admitted to rehab on anyone, but I was so glad Sue was there too. Meeting her was a blessing. Aside from the fact it meant I would have a wingman to attend meals with and a roommate with whom I could debrief, she made me look at my own situation differently.

With the possible exception of a psychopath, I couldn't imagine anyone feeling anything other than compassion for Sue on hearing about the past twelve months of her life. When she described how unsettling her cancer diagnosis had been, and how ill the chemo had made her feel, I didn't think she was weak. I didn't think she was a malingerer for having to stop work, and I certainly didn't think she was an unmitigated failure because she was unable to persevere with her daily life as if nothing was happening. It turned on some dim lightbulb in my mind that would brighten as the days passed. Perhaps I could extend some of that compassion in my own direction?

After an hour of talking, a comfortable silence hung between us. I picked up the schedule I had been given earlier and began to contemplate what my stay would entail.

The timetable for the week included individual sessions with a GP, a psychiatrist, a psychologist and a social worker, in addition to a variety of optional activities like going for a beach walk ,or taking a yoga class, or learning to meditate. There were group therapy sessions too, workshops on subjects like toxic relationships, stress management, addiction, co-dependency and family dynamics. And, of course, there were meal times.

Having had a blank schedule for months, the idea of having something to do, and somewhere to go, was invigorating. With the exception of the walks, all of these activities took place in the hospital, so it wasn't like stepping out into the real world – pyjamas were still acceptable – but it was a small move towards normality. Just the thought of having an existence that didn't revolve solely around lying on the couch made me feel better than I had in months.

My only compulsory activity on that first day was a session with the GP to touch base on my medical history.

'Certainly looks like you've had a full few years then?' he said. 'Endometriosis, Crohn's, steroids, gastroenterologists, neurologists, gynaecologists, immunosuppressants, laparoscopies …'

'What can I say? I can't get enough of the health system.'

As I exited the GP's clinic, located in another wing of the small hospital, one of the team leaders, Marcus, who had introduced himself to Sue and me earlier, was walking past and asked if I wanted to join in on the beach walk.

'It's not far, and the salty air will do you good,' he promised.

I hesitated. The last time I had attempted a proper walk had been with Nick and had ended with me in a ditch. I wasn't sure I could do it.

'It's slow,' he said. 'I'll walk with you.'

I swallowed my fear. If my vertigo *was* stress-related, as I'd started to believe it was, I had to put mind over matter. Going for a walk was probably exactly the type of thing I needed to do.

'I'll change my shoes,' I said pointing at my ballet flats.

'Great!' Marcus smiled. 'We'll all meet at the front entrance in five minutes.'

Sue was asleep when I returned to our room, so I quietly opened my cupboard to find the pair of sneakers I hadn't worn in months. At the entrance, a group of ten patients were gathered, most of whom I hadn't seen before.

'The rules are simple: we don't have to walk side by side, but we do have to stay on the same track and not lose the group,' Marcus said before he opened the door and let us out in the wild.

Some of the patients charged ahead, but I hung back. It felt quite strange being out in the open in this setting – I had barely been inside half a day, but somehow being outside like any ordinary person, without a giant label warning the world that I was an in-patient in a psychiatric hospital, felt odd.

'How long have you worked here?' I asked Marcus.

'Here? A little over a year, but I've been working in drug and alcohol rehab for fifteen years.'

'Does rehab work?'

'For who?'

'Anyone?'

'It can. Addiction is hard to cure – the number of patients who fully recover and don't ever relapse is very small, but it does happen.'

'What makes the difference?'

'The patient wanting it. You can only help yourself if you want to help yourself and you are ready.'

'Can you tell who those people are when they first come in?'

'Sometimes.'

I sped up a little to get some space and took in the idyllic view. It was a spectacular afternoon: the Pacific Ocean was literally glistening, the waves were crashing gently in unison and there wasn't a breath of wind about. The contrast between the beauty of my physical surrounds and the bleak reality of my soul felt comically stark. For most of the other beach-goers and walkers in our midst I imagine this was the backdrop to a heavenly holiday. Did they know who we were, what we were doing here?

But being outside for a walk, taking in the fresh and salty air, was exciting. Even more excitingly, there was no sign of my vertigo. I couldn't explain it – was it because I wasn't panicked?

Because I had decided to park some of my fear? For the first time in a long time I wasn't untethered from life, uncertain about what my next day would entail and fixated on whether my health would ever be returned. I realised that I felt safe. I didn't need to worry about everything. 'Everything', in my mind, was being taken care of.

I could barely bring myself to relive that last walk Nick and I had taken, only a few weeks ago, but that mental picture was so far from where I was now. From just taking steps, literally putting one foot in front of the other.

After returning and having a quick shower, I headed downstairs with Sue for dinner, which felt like a strange cross between school camp, boarding school and something entirely different.

Excruciating sadness and tangible grief were all through the room, and while there was no uniformity between and among the residents, there was some camaraderie. I was one of the younger people there – the residents' ages ranged from nineteen to seventy, and they appeared to hail from all walks of life.

That first evening, Sue and I took our seats at the end of a long empty table, which slowly filled up as our fellow residents made their way to the communal dining room. We ate with a coterie of patients from both wings, called the Jacaranda and the Jasmine wards. The former housed the patients battling addiction, the latter those with mood disorders.

There was a Jasmine gentleman who couldn't stop crying. Twice he attempted to apologise for his tears, but was unable to muster any words. He sat, broken, literally crying into his dinner. A middle-aged woman also did her best to blink back tears for the duration of dinner, but couldn't hide her distress.

At the other end of the spectrum, Steph, a lively woman in her late thirties from the Jacaranda ward, held court: captivating the table with the story of the intervention that had landed her here.

'I mean, it's not the first time they've tried,' she explained between mouthfuls of beef stroganoff. 'I hadn't answered their calls and was on an absolute bender. I mean it was solid: I hadn't been home in four days, which my flatmate ended up letting spill to my mum when she called him. Next thing, Mum had flown to Sydney and was banging on the door of my dealer and that was it.'

Every sentence ended with a contagious, throaty laugh that somehow made this turn of events seem light-hearted and funny. Even as she explained the difficult predicament she was in with her dealer, with whom she was romantically entwined, she made it somehow seem thrilling, when in reality it must have been terrifying.

'You know, it actually was pretty fucked because he was, you know, in a bit of strife and you just never knew what you'd get. Some days he was a total charmer: like I'm talking the life of any party and you just wanted to be near him and we'd party for days. But then he could turn and be fully aggressive.'

'He went sick at Mum when she turned up.' Steph laughed. 'He was just like "GET THE FUCK OUT OF HERE" but Mum couldn't give a toss. I was pretty wasted, and Mum just grabbed me by the hand and took me downstairs. My sister was waiting in the car.'

They took her back to her rented apartment in Sydney's eastern suburbs, where she slept for the rest of the day while they arranged flights back to their home on the Gold Coast and tried to get her into an in-patient program.

With an openness that amazed me, Steph talked about how

alcoholism was her biggest demon, the reason she was here, but admitted the party drugs didn't help.

'But they're so fucken fun, hey?' she said with a deep, throaty cackle that elicited chuckles all the way down the table.

I was intrigued and hung off her every word. She seemed so nonplussed about being here and confessing her troubles – it obviously wasn't her idea to come to this place, but she didn't seem to be resisting it. As she kept talking, I recalled my chat with Marcus along the beach.

Does she want to change? Will she be part of the group that beats that odds and overcomes addiction?

A few days later, news spread that Steph had led a group of Jacaranda residents off the authorised beach walking path right into the nearby surf club for drinks, thus getting them all expelled.

~

After dinner I brushed my teeth in the tiny bathroom, and changed into my pyjamas before climbing into bed. I sat up, tucked into the white sheets that had been starched as stiff as cardboard, and rang Nick, who had just finished rugby training for the night.

'How has the day been?' he asked.

'Strange,' I whispered. 'I can't explain it.'

Sue was reading in her bed just metres away with only a curtain separating us, so our conversation was short. I wanted to fill Nick in on all the intricacies of my first day but I felt shy, so after asking for an update from his world, I said I'd better go.

'Darling, are you okay?' he asked just before we hung up.

'I think so.'

And the strange part was that I meant it.

As I lay my head on the pillow I realised I was genuinely looking forward to waking up. It felt foreign. I couldn't remember the last time I had gone to sleep not dreading another day.

The drugs do work

September 2007

I was sitting in the office of the hospital director, a psychiatrist in his early fifties, whose desk was barely visible under various mountains of paper. Other than the desk, there was just a swivel chair on his side and two standard-issue office chairs on my side. No soft furnishings, and definitely no psychiatrist's couch, which I found disappointing. I could have been at a job interview.

'You say these pills aren't going to take my Crohn's away,' I said, 'and you don't think they will fix the dizziness, so how exactly are they meant to make any difference to how I *feel*?'

'They work as a circuit-breaker,' he explained. 'The type of anti-depressant you have started is called a selective serotonin reuptake inhibitor. It eases depression by increasing the levels of serotonin in the brain. Once a person is depressed, their brain is almost wired to react a certain way: once you are in that place, it's difficult to snap out of it without help in the form of both therapy, which you will undertake with Sandra, and medication.'

His office felt cramped, even with only the two of us in it. Small windows ran around the upper edge of his office walls, too high for anyone to see in, and because it was sunny outside, the space was particularly bright

'Your reservations are quite normal, Georgie. I hear them often, but this medication does work. For a lot of patients, it helps them break out of a cycle they're trapped in.'

It was obvious he'd delivered this spiel *many* times before, but it was compelling.

'That's why I'm here, isn't it?' I said. 'Anything that might break this cycle is worth trying.'

Prior to arriving at rehab I'd never taken any medication for anxiety. In fact, I had long refused to believe there was any drug in the world that could change how I – or anyone else – 'felt' in a psychological sense. It was quite a bold position, given I had absolutely no qualifications in the field and had not even familiarised myself with any scientific or academic material on the topic.

I was not dismissive about prescription drugs in general. It had never crossed my mind to knock back medication that a specialist prescribed for Crohn's disease or any other physical ailment. In later years I would quite literally tell my GP I was happy to have an epidural plugged in at any point from twelve weeks onwards, so confident was I that a highly medical birth would be right for me. (Reader, I was right.)

But when it came to matters of the mind, I was convinced that drugs couldn't help. In the same way I had clung to the idea that my vertigo was a distinct medical condition – entirely separate to my state of mind – I failed to grasp how treating anything other than the vertigo would deliver relief.

Even so, it's astounding that, until that final psychiatrist's meeting in Lismore, none of the dozens of medical professionals I met had suggested I take medication for anxiety. The most plausible explanation for this was my ridiculous fixation with appearing 'fine'. I wasn't honest. I didn't just fail to reveal my angst – I actively concealed it. I slipped into the charade of being articulate and polite the minute I walked into any medical appointment, without even trying.

I will never know whether starting an anti-depressant sooner would have circumvented some of my troubles, but I do know that starting medication helped. Enormously.

The psychiatrist at rehab explained that without these drugs I would effectively remain stuck in a hamster wheel, madly peddling without relief, wondering why the hell I still felt so hellish. That age-old definition of insanity – doing the same thing and expecting a different result – sprang to mind.

So I was prescribed three medications to treat both my anxiety and the depression that I was, by then, suffering. The first of these was the selective serotonin reuptake inhibitor (SSRI) described by the hospital director. Serotonin is one of the chemical messengers (neurotransmitters) that carry signals between brain cells. SSRIs block the reabsorption (reuptake) of serotonin into the brain, making more serotonin available, which reduces symptoms of depression and regulates anxiety. SSRIs are called 'selective' because they seem to primarily affect serotonin, not other neurotransmitters. They have fairly limited side effects.

The second and third medications I began were prescribed in combination, and were also chosen for their neurological effect. A low dose of both a beta-blocker and an old-school anti-depressant were given to me as a treatment option for vestibular migraines, which more than one neurologist had suggested was the most likely explanation for the vertigo.

I now had to accept that mental illness wasn't something that happened to 'other' people: it was happening to me. For someone seemingly capable of critical thought, I had a gigantic blind spot when it came to mental illness. I may as well have covered my ears for fifteen years and screamed, 'LALALALALALALALALA,' in the face of any suggestion that I was afflicted by anxiety.

In truth, I hadn't fully understood what anxiety was. It turned out worrying *all* the time about everything to the point I felt physically and emotionally shattered wasn't 'normal'. It was anxiety, and it needed to be treated.

While my state of denial and ignorance had its shortcomings (read earlier chapters) it had one upside: getting so unwell that I wound up in rehab meant I was effectively enrolled in an intensive course in the field of mental illness almost the minute it was identified as a (big) problem for me.

The American Psychological Association defines anxiety as 'an emotion characterised by feelings of tension, worried thoughts and physical changes like increased blood pressure.' However, there is an important distinction between normal feelings of anxiety and an anxiety disorder.

Feeling worried or stressed from time to time is absolutely to be expected: the existence of some worry is an inexorable aspect of the human condition that has been critical to our survival. Back in the day when predators and other physical dangers were constant concerns for human beings, little bursts of fear and stress served as alarms that allowed a person to take evasive action. A rush of adrenaline in response to danger will lead to a raised heartbeat, sweating and increased sensitivity to surroundings. This is known as the 'fight-or-flight' response, and it prepares humans to physically confront or flee any threats to their safety. In this way, anxiety has allowed humankind to continue. Yay!

But a spike in adrenaline is far less useful when there is no predator looming, no clear danger. Feeling a rush of stress may be useful when taking an exam, going for a job interview or even playing sport, but people with an anxiety disorder are very generous – profligate even – with their worries. They do not limit them to the rare occasion they find themselves being chased by a tiger, or even to exams. Instead they feel anxious and worried almost *all* of the time.

For me, a racing mind, fast-beating heart, sweaty palms, wrenching gut and surging adrenaline were not special-occasion sensations: they were merely conditions for living. For a psychiatrist, this was proof that I was in the clutches of an anxiety disorder.

I had long spent my days effectively living in fear of a predator that didn't exist, but anxiety was the actual predator that I needed to confront. It was genuinely mind-boggling to consider that I might be able to exist without intense and persistent fears.

Anxiety has become something of a buzzword. In Sarah Wilson's bestselling book on the subject, *First We Make the Beast Beautiful*, she notes that before 1950 there were only two books published on anxiety. Now, if you search for 'anxiety' online, you can choose from thousands and thousands of titles. Anxiety disorders are the most common mental illness in America, affecting an estimated 40 million adults aged eighteen and older, or 18.1 per cent of the population every year. In Australia it affects roughly one in seven of us each year. Of these, it's estimated that just under three per cent experience generalised anxiety disorder (GAD), like I did. But nearly six per cent of the population will experience GAD at some time in their lifetime. Women are slightly more likely than men to be afflicted; it can occur at any time in life and is common in all age groups, including among children and older people.

Those little percentages weren't reflected in the rehab population though: we were *all* suffering. Each night after dinner, a long queue would form at the nurses' station as we all waited to have our drugs divvied out for the evening. I would be handed a small paper cup with six tablets: some, like the white prednisone pills that I'd been on for years, were familiar. Others, like the two pink ones, were new. The nurse on duty would have to watch us physically swallow whatever pills we were given to ensure we didn't skip – or stash – the medication we'd been prescribed. Each time, just before I'd down my tablets with a small gulp of water, I'd hesitate.

Am I going to feel better? Is a flood of Zen going to rush through my body? Will I feel anything?

Of course it didn't work like that. There was no magic. I simply swallowed them, walked to my room and went to bed.

I didn't begin my anti-anxiety tablets on the Monday and wake up on Tuesday feeling like a whole new person. But it didn't take too long to realise I was feeling different.

~

'Close your eyes and get settled in your chair,' Marcus began. 'Pay attention to how your body feels on the chair. Move to a position that is comfortable. Let your arms relax. Lay your hands in your lap or by your side. Whatever feels best.'

His voice was soothing and calm. The room was cool, the blinds were drawn and the eucalyptus trees just outside rustled gently in the wind. I was about to embark on my first breathing class. Who knew that was something I needed to learn?

The fact I was here was notable, but the fact my heart wasn't racing was even better. Up until this point I had viewed yoga, exercise and relaxation as luxuries that those in the grips of busy stressful jobs simply did not have time for. I laughed alongside my fellow legal graduates after we were told in our induction week that we had access to a gym membership: when exactly would any of us have time to go to the gym?

On the odd occasion I did take yoga classes, I found them to be anxiety-inducing. Spending any time 'alone' in my head was hell on a plate, and attempting to conjure a still mind literally triggered panic. So having little time for yoga had probably been a blessing, but putting self-care at the bottom of my to-do list was not.

I will go for a walk when this six-week deal is finally done. I will set aside time for 'relaxation' after this rotation. I will see a psychologist just as soon as I deteriorate so badly that I am temporarily institutionalised.

I had my wires crossed badly.

If the body is a temple, at rehab I discovered that mine had long been defaced. And I resented it. While I hadn't prioritised my physical wellbeing, I also hadn't abused it. I wasn't drinking heavily, taking drugs, relying on pain killers, avoiding sleep, starving myself or engaging in any destructive habits. At the time the fact these weren't among my problems fed into my frustration about feeling so unwell.

How can one person's body withstand days of abuse without disintegrating, while eating a piece of bread can floor me?

It was infuriating.

Even with my illnesses I had expected myself to be physically capable of doing whatever I wanted, whenever I wanted. I believed the absence of any obviously toxic habits should by right translate into some broad insurance policy. The loophole was that my wanton negligence of my overall health and the constant state of stress I occupied *was* a toxic habit.

In an information session on anxiety I had learned about the close physical connection between breathing and the condition. In Marcus's breathing classes, I came to *feel* how my breathing was linked to my state of mind. I had been a lifetime shallow-breather. It was all I had ever known, and thinking about changing that made my breath even shallower. For as long as I could remember, every ninth or tenth breath I took required me to inhale deeply enough to scale what felt like a mini mountain inside my chest.

When I was particularly worried or stressed, this would happen more frequently, at which point the cycle would feed itself. Feeling anxious triggered shortness of breath and shallow breathing, but shortness of breath and shallow breathing also triggered feeling anxious. Being able to tune into this and consciously slow down my breath allowed to me seize control: I could let the adrenaline dissipate and slow the panic. I could make myself feel better, and not in a distant, hypothetical 'by-eating-kale-I-will-add-five-years-to-my-life' sense.

Doing precisely the kind of uber-peaceful yoga classes I had always considered an absurd, panic-inducing waste of time was similarly restorative. It felt good to take care of myself, not because I was smugly ticking something off a list, but because it literally *felt* good. The pleasure in using my body, even gently, was profound. In these yoga classes I started to relish the sensation of being at peace, of slowing my mind, of actively letting go of my thoughts and worries.

Between yoga and breathing classes at rehab it became obvious, physically, that 'relaxation' wasn't just an irritating, well-intended suggestion so much as a necessary skill. And it wasn't something that I could foist upon myself only once I identified a spare forty-five minutes in a week and decided to *relax, goddammit*.

When I think back now to the months before the vertigo set in, I was like a car with a flat battery. With a jump start and a lot of effort I could just about putter around the block, but it wasn't effortless or pretty, and with each trip the next journey became less viable. I had been running on empty for so long that it was a miracle I was able to start at all. Which is why, eventually, I couldn't.

I got to twenty-five years of age without knowing how to breathe properly. This was huge. It made me not only academically understand what Dr Wagner had said about stress having a physical impact on the body, but made me *feel* it. It was a tangible example of the physical ramifications of anxiety.

And it was something I could influence.

~

One afternoon, before I had an appointment with my new psychologist, Sandra, I walked downstairs to the little gym that I had been shown when I first arrived. I wanted to do something, and I had realised that each time I did gentle activity, I felt good. The 'gym' was really just a large room, naturally lit thanks to large glass doors running along the back wall, dotted with a few unintimidating pieces of exercise equipment. It could have been someone's living room. There were yoga mats and several sets of small hand-weights lined up in one corner. I picked out one of the mats and unfolded it on the floor.

I lay down, closed my eyes and practised the breathing exercise Marcus had taught me a few days earlier. For ten minutes I just enjoyed being still, breathing in and out, relaxing. I didn't feel panicked or worried. I actually loved being still. Afterwards I sat on an exercise bike and gently cycled for another ten minutes. I didn't do enough to break a sweat, but I was moving my body and it felt good. I didn't feel weak or dizzy, and I wasn't nervously awaiting either sensation.

The world didn't seem so desperately dark.

This change in perspective, after months of gloom, felt quietly enormous. Since I didn't have another version of myself living in a parallel setting to run a double blind test, I have no way of knowing whether the drugs alone caused it or whether it was the combination of the drugs and the mental reboot that rehab forced upon me. I suspect, and I might be wrong, that even if I had commenced the medication but returned to my old life without making some of the changes rehab set in motion, my old habits might have returned. But I'll never know for sure.

What I do know is that I am still on those drugs, and ten years on they still work. All three were deemed safe enough to continue through pregnancy and breastfeeding, so I have literally been on them non-stop for more than a decade. On the odd occasions when I have skipped them – because I've either forgotten to take them or run out – I quite quickly feel dreadful enough to I accept I'll likely take them for the rest of my life. I can accept that without any qualms, because in me, they obviously address some type of imbalance that I'm not sure anything other than medication could help.

In weeks and months to come, the wonder-tablet for anxiety wove its magic and eased the physical intensity of a burden I hadn't realised I carried. It was like coming inside after a month camping in the rain to a toasty house, a hot shower, clean PJs and a bowl of soup. But the relief was even sweeter, because despite being effectively drenched and shivering, I hadn't even realised I had been caught in the rain.

You are what you think

September 2007

'If I were a cow, I definitely would have been put down, or put out to pasture at best,' I said. 'I am broken. Faulty goods. What's the point in someone like me pretending otherwise?'

I was in my first one-on-one session with Sandra, a psychologist with a mop of raven curls perched in a messy bun on the top of her head. She had been charged with lifting the lid of my mind, a task I imagine was akin to a mechanic opening the bonnet of a car only to discover a knot of a thousand elastic bands sitting where the engine ought to have been.

'I'm not convinced that's a helpful comparison,' she said, looking me right in the eyes. 'You weren't bred for human consumption or to produce milk.'

'Mmm.' I shrugged.

'Okay then,' Sandra said, changing tack and putting her notes down. 'How would you define a human being's value or worth?'

'When everything works,' I said.

'Do you think "everything works" in every person of value?'

'Well, I think when nothing works there is no value.'

'So *that* – things working – is the sum of a human being's value?'

'No, I would say a human's value goes beyond that, but when nothing works – and nothing works in me – it's a moot point.'

'Okay,' she said resignedly. 'We're going to have daily sessions together while you're here, and I think we'll really concentrate on unpacking some of the thought patterns that are contributing to how you're feeling. Have you heard of cognitive behavioural therapy? CBT?'

'I can't say I have, no.'

'When I see you tomorrow I'll tell you more about it and we can get started. I think it will really help.'

Even though I had no idea what CBT was, I liked knowing I would see Sandra the next day, and I especially liked that she had a plan. The realisation that I wasn't being left to my own devices in searching for a solution to my problems was steadying. I had done fragmented care, ably pieced together by Mum, without much luck for months, and between appointments I had been drifting and lost. No single doctor or professional seemed willing or able to take the lead on looking after me. My split life between Lismore and Sydney made that even more unlikely. Being in one place where everything was lined up, where my carers and doctors were integrated, working as a team and singing from the same song sheet, was of inestimable value. I needed to immerse myself in care, and rehab gave me the pool.

Plato famously defined thinking as talking to one's own soul. In embarking upon the process of changing my thinking – CBT, to give it the technical label – with Sandra, it became evident that the trash-talk I had fed my soul until this point would have been enough to make the very late Plato roll in his grave. It was certainly enough to push me right to the brink.

Sandra was right when she said CBT could be a game-changer for me. While medication can treat the symptoms of an anxiety disorder, therapy helps to tackle the underlying cause of the problem and manage it in very practical ways. Before, I had naively assumed therapy was only for people who had suffered some serious form of trauma – abuse, neglect, grief. It turned out the bit where all my thoughts revolved around the idea I was valueless meant therapy *could* be of benefit to me. And I was far from being laughed off Sandra's couch: she practically locked me in her room.

'Even in the absence of any objective hardship or trauma, patients can develop problematic thinking patterns that shape their world in less than ideal ways,' she said. 'Sometimes this can make patients feel miserable and sick. CBT is an evidence-based form of psychological therapy that helps you to change your thinking and behaviour by tuning in and challenging the stories you might not even realise you are telling yourself.'

'I didn't even know that was possible?'

'It is. And it can be quite powerful. The way you think determines how you feel, and distorted thinking patterns can trigger and exacerbate feelings of distress. When a person is in the thick of generalised anxiety, their thinking pattern can become chronically distorted, which compounds the distress.'

CBT examines the way we look at the world and ourselves: it's a combination of cognitive therapy, which examines how negative thoughts, or cognitions, contribute to anxiety, and behavioural therapy, which examines how you behave in situations that trigger anxiety. Together? It's really something. Which is why

I'm not surprised research concludes that CBT produces the most consistent results of any treatment (including medication) for anxiety sufferers the world over.

Sandra taught me that my thoughts – more than external events – affect the way I feel. It's not the situation a person is in that determines how they feel so much as their perception of the situation. This is why an invitation to a fabulous party will inspire excitement and joy for some people, while in others it will trigger so much fear and foreboding that they immediately adopt the foetal position.

Ostensibly the situation – being invited to a party – is identical for each person, but the perception of it, and the resulting emotions, can and will differ wildly. Those of us inclined towards anxiety are likely to feel fear and foreboding far more reflexively than we feel excitement or happiness, regardless of the precise situation, which is where CBT can help.

But it requires work. CBT dispelled the misconception I had that 'therapy' would involve lying on a couch casually reaching for whatever dark secret first leaped to mind. It was the equivalent of turning up to a lecture only to discover it was actually a student-led tutorial, and I was the student in charge. It required real buy-in, quite a bit of homework and far less of the casual wallowing I had always assumed sessions with a shrink would entail.

We are all creatures of habit, and the narrative loop inside our minds is quite often just an automated response that we have accepted as gospel. It might not be true, but we've repeated it so often that it may as well be. CBT requires the creation of a new habit: of effectively pausing to contemplate a thought and verifying it against some measure of logic before accepting it as truth.

Sandra helped me discover I had a tendency towards selective thinking (I focused exclusively on my flaws), magnification (I was certain those flaws were gigantic) and personalisation (everything was my fault). And at the root of my mental discontent was one pervasive automatic thought that was largely based around the idea that I was hopeless and utterly worthless.

'Have you ever considered whether this conclusion you've reached, this idea that you're hopeless or worthless, is actually based on any evidence?' Sandra asked me once. 'Often we take things as fact when they are actually just assumptions. In psychology we call these "distorted thoughts". If you've started from the assumption that you're hopeless, it will take very little to confirm that theory for you.'

She explained that this might be why, for me, the need for one sick day was tantamount to being publicly revealed as a failure. I could get from A to B so quickly I didn't even realise I'd been on a journey.

As I mulled over this possibility, the pieces started to fall into place. I had to admit, it would explain why I had so often felt desperately inadequate and inferior. At school and university, I had been one of those deeply annoying people who assumed, before every exam and assignment, that this would be the one I'd screw up. Given my track record of *not* failing this was, understandably, maddening for my friends. 'Why go through this bloody routine every time?' they often asked.

Now I understood. It wasn't rational, and it wasn't a plea for reassurance. It was the inevitable consequence of genuinely believing I was hopeless.

My CBT sessions – in rehab and beyond – always began with a discussion of what worries had been dominating my mind. This was never difficult because, even now, if left to my own devices I can very easily fret away the rest of my existence. Worry is the safe harbour my mind will always sail towards. At rehab, my work and my illness were two interrelated concerns that were, unsurprisingly, a source of considerable angst. While at uni, I had been able to manage my workload and illness privately because of the relative autonomy study offered. Even before I began full-time work, I was acutely aware that being sick was going to be difficult to reconcile with my professional obligations. (My professional obligations were also going to be difficult to reconcile with my physical symptoms, but, funnily enough, that wasn't how I looked at it.)

Each time I suffered some episode due to my Crohn's, my mental process went something along these lines:

I have a chronic illness.

I'm not good enough for this job.

I'm hopeless.

It's just a matter of time before I lose my job and am unemployed for the rest of my life.

I am a total failure, and soon the whole world will discover this truth that I've been hiding.

If I had, by some miracle, seen that thought process laid out in that way at the time, it's possible I would have been able to recognise the holes in the logic. But it happened so fast I didn't have time to unpack it – I didn't even know it had happened. All I knew was that I felt dread the minute I felt unwell, which compounded my physical symptoms.

In one of our CBT sessions, Sandra suggested we unpack the prevailing idea that I wasn't really worthy of my job.

'What grounds do you have to believe you are unfit to be working as a lawyer?'

Channelling the solicitor from *The Castle*, I explained it was just 'the vibe': 'There's no single reason, I suppose. More some feelings. I wasn't very robust. I didn't come from a law-ish family. I didn't really understand trusts. I wasn't as smart as everyone else.'

'To reach a conclusion you plan to rely on, you need to show actual grounds,' Sandra said, which reminded me rather a lot of my law exams. (The ones I sat in order to obtain the degree that made me qualified to work as a junior solicitor.) 'Having graduated from the necessary degree and gone through a recruitment process to obtain a job is irrefutable proof that, objectively, you are qualified for the job,' she said. 'Whether you want that job, like that job or are suited to the job are different questions, but being unworthy or unqualified is not up for debate.'

These sessions unpicking my thoughts revealed that I was very rarely actually 'thinking' when I devalued myself: I was just doing.

Sandra set me an exercise for homework.

'I want you to go away and think about how you would describe a meaningful life. What would it involve? How would it feel? What would make it meaningful?'

After dinner I sat up in my starchy single bed with my hospital-issued notebook and started to write down some ideas. I started to visualise how a meaningful life might look and feel to me, and I imagined freeing myself of the fear and self-loathing I hadn't realised were optional. It was unfamiliar and novel to consider the future in positive terms. My heart started racing at the very thought. I pictured myself waking up without dread. No knot in my stomach, no apprehension, no angst.

When I started, even hypothetically, imagining that I was not hopeless, that I was worthy, my outlook started to shift. I came to enjoy picking through my memories, mentally road-testing how

I might have felt about these scenarios if I'd come at them from a different starting point. I couldn't describe all the trimmings of a meaningful life, but I did know that a life in which I didn't constantly berate myself was appealing.

I was becoming acutely aware of the things I was fortunate to have in my corner – options, family, love, friendship and, perhaps, in time, even health. I began imagining how my days might feel if my starting point was closer to 'you are enough' than 'you are useless'. Could I fake it till I made it my normal?

I remembered a farewell gathering at the law firm, halfway through my graduate program, when a senior lawyer in the group was leaving to become a partner at another firm. Her speech was short but refreshingly truthful, which is why I could recall the opening so vividly. She had been working at the firm for over a decade, and had been a senior associate for more than enough years to have become a partner, and yet it hadn't happened.

'There comes a point in everyone's life, and certainly in their working life, where *you* have to back yourself. Where you wake up and start believing in your ability.'

I was struck by her bravery: even when the firm she had worked so hard for, for her whole career, didn't see fit to promote her to partner, she decided to back herself anyway and find a firm that would. I remember thinking how clever she was. Having that pluck meant she would realise her career dream. The alternative would be defeat, beavering away in a firm that wouldn't promote her.

At that time, the foundations of my self-worth were firmly predicated on external benchmarks. If I had been that senior lawyer, and the firm I wanted to work at didn't pick me to be partner, any self-belief I had would have collapsed. I wouldn't have had the courage to pursue other options.

When I put my mind to it, I could see that illness and a life of meaning were not mutually exclusive. Far from it. But until I invested some time into breaking the habitual conclusion that I had less value as a person because I was ill, I wouldn't be able to believe it.

~

One simple but effective 'trick' Sandra taught me at rehab was doing a mental inventory every night before I went to sleep. When I laid my head on the pillow, I had to think of three things I did that day that had made me laugh or feel happy, proud or positive. Finding three things – no matter how inconsequential – that made me feel good, satisfied or productive distracted my mind from all the things I didn't do. The things that made me feel guilty or worried or scared.

It was a surprisingly easy habit to develop once I put my mind to it, because it felt good and it had a flow-on effect. Throughout the day I would catch myself subconsciously searching for the good things – the potential pluses – I could happily dwell on at night. Though subtle, this pivoting of my paradigm was significant.

Comradeship

September 2007

'Not today,' John said, tears streaming down his face, which was crumpled with pain. Seven of us were sitting in a circle of armchairs in a cosy carpeted room for group therapy. I'd seen John at the table the night before. He was so depressed that he couldn't meet another person's eyes without tears tumbling down his face, so overcome with sadness that he could barely speak. His body mirrored his state of mind: crestfallen.

'That's fine, John,' said Victoria, the warm psychologist leading the session. 'You just let me know if you do want to speak.'

Victoria had invited us each to introduce ourselves and explain, in our own words, what had been going on and what we wanted to achieve in rehab. After five of my fellow inmates had shared their experiences, it was my turn.

'I have had a tough few months,' I started. 'Actually it's probably been longer than that. I can't really remember when I last felt well.

'I moved to Sydney last year after finishing uni and I started a graduate job, but it didn't really work out that well. I just kept getting sick. And I found it so stressful because I couldn't hide being sick, so I wasn't any good at my job. I didn't even really like my job, but I hated that I couldn't do it. I hated feeling so hopeless.'

I felt like I was in a fishbowl, with all of my inner demons and vulnerabilities plain for everyone to see, but inexplicably, I wasn't mortified. I had never openly revealed the extent of my pain for fear of the picture it painted and yet I did so in a room full of strangers. Perhaps it was because I could also see the demons and vulnerabilities of others so plainly?

As we left the session and dispersed in different directions, John came up to me.

'Don't you be sad, love,' he said. 'There's so much for you.'

His sincerity and compassion were piercing. It was the only sentence he spoke without crying for the duration of my stay. I wanted to wrap my arms around this kind, wounded soul and make him better.

How can humans be so broken?

~

After being so physically dependent on Mum for months, it was restorative to feel a semblance of independence and to participate in a version of life. I approached my schedule with vigour and attended virtually every single organised activity – including turning up to a narcotics anonymous session purely because it was on, and staying for the entire thing because it was too fascinating to leave. Admittedly it was awkward at the end when everyone was asked to share something of their experience with addiction and I scrambled to explain that addiction wasn't exactly my chief problem.

I sat in sessions and workshops with my jaw on the floor:

why had I never learned the fundamentals of a healthy mind? Why had it never occurred to me that I had some autonomy over how I thought? And how I felt? I was properly honest with every professional I saw – after all, the game was up by this point. Suddenly the roots of my troubles, hidden for so long, were plain to see. *I* was lifting the lid on the bonnet and for the first time *seeing* why I wasn't able to function.

In the crash-course in mental illness that was my stint in rehab, the material on offer was not just theoretical, either. Living with fifty residents in the throes of various conditions and illnesses of the mind was a rather efficient way to grasp the practical realities of mental illness. It was also, often, desperately sad.

Other than a few of the residents in for substance abuse, who seemed to primarily have a penchant for too much fun, most of the in-patients seemed to be temporarily trapped outside of life, unable to experience fun at all. The effects of mental illness were laid bare in all of their undeniable physiological gore.

Of course there was John, unable to stop himself from crying. He had a family who visited regularly. He was retired and he had a 'good' life. He wasn't destitute or abandoned or heartbroken: there was no 'reason' for his depression, a fact that only added to his pain. He hated himself for feeling the way he did as much as he hated the feeling itself, and in this regard he was like many of the men and women we were living alongside.

Tania was the walking wounded, but her scar tissue was hidden. She worked in a managerial position at a big public hospital before being paralysed by an acute episode of depression. She had suffered before, but not like this. Just a few weeks earlier, she had been carrying out a stressful role, capable and confident, responsible for scores of patients and staff, and now she struggled to get out of bed. On the rare occasions she ventured out of her room, she was left shattered. Brushing her hair and changing out of her pyjamas required energy she didn't have.

'How did this happen?' she once asked in disbelief in a group session. 'I don't know how I ever did it. I don't know what changed.'

Her angst was palpable and painful to watch. What did change?

There were teachers, mechanics, builders and white-collar office workers like me. In some cases there were obvious 'triggers' – job losses, relationship breakdowns, addiction, illness – but in lots of cases there was no precipitating event. Mental illness had taken hold, and there was no oxygen left for anything else.

Each time Tania spoke, I was reminded of a famous legal case that involved the concept of a skull like an eggshell. It set the precedent that if you punch someone, even gently, and it cracks their skull, you are still responsible for the full extent of the injuries they suffer, even if you believed a little nudge to the head wouldn't hurt. It doesn't matter if the same punch would barely leave a bruise on another person. If the individual you choose to punch happens to have a skull that disintegrates on contact, like an eggshell might, you are responsible for the damage.

I thought of this in rehab often. It occurred to me that what might send me into a spiral of despair would barely cause a ripple in another person, and while that could be maddening, it was the way things were. There was no logical explanation for why Tania could withstand her stressful job one week and couldn't the next. As human beings we are all wired differently: we have different dispositions, different thresholds, different triggers, and these are not static. Even as individuals, what we can withstand one week is not necessarily the same as what we can withstand the next.

This was liberating to accept. My CBT sessions were beginning to make me question everything I had taken for granted, and that included the very particular brand of shame that hangs around anyone who has crumpled under the pressure of ordinary life. As tempting as it is to fixate on whether something *ought* to legitimately cause angst or not, or whether you have any grounds to be depressed or suffer anxiety, there comes a point where the damage needs more scrutiny than the punch – or events – that preceded it. Once a skull is shattered, that's the bit that needs attention.

Observing a large group of effectively shattered skulls up-close provided something of a reality check that I'm not sure anything else could have delivered. But accepting that your mental illness is simply a fact of life isn't easy. Virtually everyone at rehab described an extraordinary weight of guilt and angst about their condition, over and above the condition itself. Everyone hated themselves for feeling the way they did. They hated letting their families or their workplaces or their partners or their kids down. They hated causing problems. They hated being a problem. They all wished it would go away. Some of them very genuinely wished themselves away.

As my cohabitants wrapped words around their grief and guilt, I wanted to interrupt.

It's not your fault you're unwell. You are doing your best! All you need to do is control what you can. Focus on getting as well as you can and everything else can wait. Stop beating yourself up!

If the words pot, kettle and black spring to mind at this point, I hear you. Lord, do I hear you. Who was *I* to admonish anyone for crunching salt into their own open wounds?

This whole reflected perspective is the reason I think group therapy – wildly confronting in theory but strangely comforting in practice – worked for me. In these sessions we had the chance to respond to one another, and ten times out of ten the responses offered were along the lines of what I had wanted to say – along the lines of what each of us could well have said to ourselves: cut yourself a break. We were all dealing with enough without heaping mountains of unnecessary shit on the top.

Perfectionism is a fast track to misery

September 2007

If you wanted to make your life better what is the one thing you'd change?

Eliminate fear.

I was sitting up on my bed, using a meal tray as my desk, staring at those two little words. It was just after lunch and I had two free hours before my next appointment. The eucalyptus trees were swaying gently outside, and the sky was an unblemished expanse of blue. I stood up and pushed my window ajar to feel the fresh air. Sue was out, so I had the room to myself.

The question about making my life better had been posed at the end of a group therapy session earlier, and my answer, underlined in my notebook in lead pencil, shocked me.

I was scared *all the time*.

What was I so afraid of? Failing? Being disliked? Being seen as inadequate or incompetent? Did these things even matter? Why was I holding myself hostage to fear?

Even *thinking* about a life without fear felt thrilling. I thought about Sal, one of my housemates in Darlinghurst, who I had envied desperately when we lived together. She was so relaxed and unfazed by life, happily meandering through her days with incredible ease. We all joked that she was so laid-back it was a wonder she was standing. Sal didn't spend her every waking moment fretting, and nothing disastrous eventuated because of it. On the contrary, it seemed a terrifically enjoyable way of life, but at the time, me being more like her seemed wholly inconceivable.

But it was something I thought about often. Sal and I had started living together at the same time that I had started full-time work, which was around the time I had begun quite actively expecting a change in myself. I'd finished five and a half years of university and had quietly assumed that the weight I had grown accustomed to lugging around on my shoulders throughout my years of study would lift. I had finally graduated and got a good job. All that was left was to go to work and get on with my life.

But the load didn't budge. It was as heavy as ever. I began wondering if anything I achieved would ever be good enough, and the answer that kept cropping up was no.

I didn't know there was a name for that paradigm at the time, but I had an inkling that something in my way of living was a little awry. Enlightenment came in a workshop on perfectionism run by Victoria, a psychologist I'd come to know through the group therapy sessions she ran.

'We are going to explore perfectionism today, and before we begin I want to get a sense from you about how it might be impacting each of you,' she said to kick things off. There were eight of us sitting at a group of desks, representatives from both the Jacaranda and the Jasmine wards, and she was standing up the front. We could have been at a uni tutorial.

'Put your hand up if you have ever felt like nothing you do is good enough,' Victoria asked.

I practically snorted, inadvertently, as I shot up my hand. Several other hands went up too.

Victoria looked at me with a smile. 'Georgie, my question obviously struck something in you. When can you remember feeling that way?'

'My whole life. I have literally never *not* felt that way.'

A man in his forties laughed. 'Me too,' he said.

'That's not an unusual response in here,' Victoria said. 'Perfectionism is a pervasive risk factor for depression and anxiety, so it's an issue for many patients.' Clinical perfectionism, she explained, is described as relentlessly striving for high achievements and unfairly judging yourself when those goals can't be met. 'For perfectionists,' she went on, 'life is an endless report card, and anything less than an A+ is a failure. And the trouble is no one ever gets A+ for everything, and life isn't a subject at school. Failure in some form or another is inevitable. But for perfectionists, falling short, even in little ways, can feel catastrophic.'

To say I related is an understatement.

I had always thought 'I'm a perfectionist' was a humblebrag: shorthand for 'I have impeccably high standards', 'I work hard', 'I pursue excellence'. Why else was it relied upon so often in response to that age-old interview question: What are your weaknesses?

In recruitment, I had learned, framing a penchant for details and excellent results as a 'flaw' ticked a few boxes: it lets you recognise your own 'shortcomings' while leaving the impression you were driven and focused. Personally, I used it on several occasions, and while it may have helped land me a few jobs, in rehab I learned the joke was on me.

Perfectionism was my paradigm.

'One of the reasons perfectionism is toxic is because ultimately it's about seeking the approval of others,' Victoria said. 'It's about measuring up, but perfectionists rarely concede that they do measure up.'

The penny dropped. Being 'perfect' was the armour I sought out to protect myself from falling short. I was living at the mercy of what I imagined 'other people' thought, and not because I was particularly invested in the views of any person in particular. I was terrified of being judged by *anyone* about *anything*.

When Victoria asked us to reflect on a time where we could recall perfectionism impacting us, my mind immediately turned to what I had always found a strange source of angst for me: casual Fridays at the law firm.

Monday through Thursday, I rarely gave much thought to what I wore, thanks to the rigid corporate dress code. On Fridays, however, we were free to mix it up within the bounds of 'smart-casual in a professional setting'. And every Friday morning that vague description would send me into a spiral. I would pull out item after item in a mad attempt to find some combination that would satisfy all the criteria in my head, angrily discarding them one by one because they all looked and felt *wrong*.

I would stand in front of the mirror, surrounded by a growing pile of shoes, shirts and jeans, barely able to contain my despair and humiliation. I usually enjoyed clothes, but I hated those mornings viscerally, not least because I couldn't quite understand why I was behaving in this way.

The truth was that I was desperate for the approval of my peers, and that desperation made me certain that nothing I owned looked even remotely good enough.

Even thinking about those dreaded mornings now makes my skin crawl. I would work myself into a total state.

Why did it matter? Why did I care? Why did I hate myself so much?

The strange phenomena of a woman having a wardrobe full of clothes with nothing to wear is hardly a worthy crisis – I knew that even then – but what I didn't appreciate was that the battle I was waging on those dreaded mornings wasn't superficial. I was experiencing an existential crisis triggered by the fact it was the only day of the week where I had some leeway to express myself. This was completely overwhelming, because I didn't know who I was. All I knew was that I needed to look a certain way, and no matter how hard I tried, I couldn't achieve it.

The issue was not the clothes or even my body. No outfit was ever going to feel right enough, because I wanted an outfit that would make me feel perfect, at a time when I had never felt less perfect.

Tal Ben-Shahar is a renowned Harvard University professor who describes himself as a 'recovering perfectionist'. In his twenties he was an accomplished athlete and a brilliant student, but he was wracked with an intense fear of failure that made him anxious and desperately unhappy. One winter day in 1999, he experienced what he had feared the most: he got a B. It triggered a personal crisis that he has been effectively researching ever since. Much of that work confirmed what his personal experience taught him: perfectionism makes people miserable.

The perfectionistic mindset can infect all aspects of life

– grades, careers, relationships and physical appearance. 'This schema enters into our cognition, and we start to accept it,' Ben-Shahar writes. 'You're either on a perfect diet or you're fat. You're either a supermodel or you're overweight.'

Two immutable facts of life make this paradigm calamitous: perfection is impossible to achieve, and failure is inevitable. Getting so sick that I had to retreat from life and be admitted to a psychiatric hospital was a powerful lesson in both.

Victoria helped me to recognise how perfectionism had contributed to my undoing. The reason I hadn't stopped to prioritise my health earlier was that ultimately, I was scared doing that meant failure. Doing *anything* outside what I perceived as the 'norm' for highly functioning individuals was failure.

'Very few people *like* failure, but getting comfortable with it will make life a lot easier, because it is going to happen,' Victoria said. 'That doesn't mean giving up or bowing out from trying hard things. It means accepting that no path is perfectly linear and that deviations will happen.'

She explained that it's the perception of, and reaction to 'failure' that makes perfectionism toxic. In the binary land of the perfectionist mind, the expectation is that every path will be smooth and easy to navigate, and when that isn't the case, coping is difficult.

'Consider a married couple,' Victoria said. 'For a perfectionist, having a fight can be hugely unsettling because they are likely to perceive it as either a failure on their part or in their marriage. The truth is, spouses arguing and facing tension is a perfectly normal occurrence in most relationships. Obviously there will be times when a couple fighting isn't perfectly normal, but no relationship can survive the pressure to be entirely tension-free.'

To challenge the perfectionist mindset, Victoria recommended the same practical exercise that Sandra had suggested: thinking of three things, no matter how small, that had happened that day which made us feel *something* positive: happy, proud, grateful, relieved.

'The point of this exercise is to develop a new habit in your thinking to focus on the positives in your day and foster gratitude,' she said. 'It's simple but very powerful, because it forces you to think differently. It can chip away at the tendency perfectionists have to be highly critical of themselves.'

For a long time, the list I had mentally scrolled through before I went to sleep each night had contained far more than three items, none of them positive. My mind would swirl through everything I had ever done wrong. I could just as readily fret about the work email I hadn't sent that day as I could ruminate over a fight I'd had with my sister in 1996. I could flit between worrying about the exercise I hadn't done or the financial plan that I hadn't actioned, to the concept I didn't fully understand at work, to scrutinising my credentials as a friend, sister, daughter, girlfriend, lawyer, human.

Because this stressful bedtime habit was as familiar to me as it was entrenched, the exercise Sandra and Victoria prescribed stuck out as something worth trying.

Imagine falling asleep focusing on something good? Not being consumed with fear? Is that even possible?

I was learning that it was.

That night as I tucked myself in, I was looking forward to putting this activity to the test. I was strict and didn't let my mind wander. I started to think about what had happened that day that had made me *feel* good.

I thought of the walk I took along the beach before dinner, a new habit, and about the thrill I'd felt at being outside. I thought of the group therapy session in which I had been honest, again, about what I was feeling, and about how strangely rewarding it felt to be vulnerable: to actually own my quirks instead of desperately trying to hide them.

I thought about the conversation I'd had with Nick before I hopped into bed. About how lucky and happy I was to have this warm, kind and funny person in my life.

I wasn't yet ready to reach for things I had *done* well, but I was able to latch on to the parts of my day that had left me feeling good.

Feeling, for once, more content than afraid, I drifted into sleep.

~

The next day, feeling motivated after the success of the positive thinking exercise, I sat at one of the small tables in the common room after lunch to do some CBT homework Sandra had set. The worksheet she had given me had three columns running vertically down the page, with headings on the top on each that read: *Identify negative thoughts, Address distortions in thoughts* and *Generate more positive thoughts.*

Thought-challenging was the object of this exercise and Sandra was going to work through my answers at our next session. She suggested I identify a negative thought that I had grappled with in the period leading up to the first vertigo episode. When it came to finding negative thoughts I had a natural advantage: there were so many to choose from.

I settled on a line of thinking that was on high rotation before I really fell apart.

Identify negative thought

You will get fired because you are sick and took today off work. No one else has as many sick days as you do. You are a lazy failure who doesn't deserve a job. You will never get better.

For a person not in the throes of an anxiety disorder, needing a sick day is unlikely to trigger an existential crisis, spark fear of getting fired or genuinely threaten one's sense of validity. For me, though, sick days did all of that.

There were a few separate occasions when my Crohn's was so bad that my specialist admitted me to hospital, and even then the worst part was not my bleeding bowel or the excruciating pain of my perpetually-enraged digestive tract: it was the self-loathing that engulfed me because of it. I almost wilfully overlooked the biological realities of my condition and instead honed in on the myriad grounds I had for detesting myself.

On these days I quite literally personified a nervous wreck: I was edgy, uptight and frazzled. My heart palpated to the point of causing nausea, my fingers picked incessantly at whatever nails or flesh they could find, and almost as soon as the day began, I would fret about the next day and the day after that and the day after that. Feeling unwell on a Tuesday immediately and invariably sparked an intensely consuming fear about Wednesday and Thursday and Friday.

Will you ever not feel unwell? Will you need the whole week off? They probably think you are faking it. You probably are faking it. No one else needs sick days like you do.

On days like these, I remember contemplating what seemed to me an extraordinary feat: the existence of individuals who could 'fake' the odd sick day without being gripped by agitation or unease. Were we even the same species?

I was not imagining it: some people really were free from the perpetual fear that dogged my existence. For those with anxiety disorders, situations are invariably perceived as more dangerous than they really are. It's like a perverse party trick – we can see danger lurking where others can't! We can find reasons to conjure dread where none exists!

While this creates a number of actual life problems, at least it provides excellent fodder for CBT. I moved on to the next column.

Address distortions in those thoughts

You are sick; human beings get sick. You have a chronic illness so you do get sick more than other people. When you are not sick, you are a hard worker.

One of the tenets of CBT is to evaluate – and troubleshoot – your panic-provoking thoughts. It involved questioning the assumptions I'd made that formed the basis of my fears, and testing out the reality of my negative predictions.

Will I really be fired? Am I really lazy? Do I really not deserve a job because I have a chronic illness?

Unpicking this, even in hindsight, was instructive. To my delight, I discovered that after A, being sick, I could reach other conclusions besides B, I am a worthless, attention-seeking malingerer. It quite genuinely opened up a whole new world.

Who knew being rational and open-minded to one's self was possible? After learning to engage in CBT, I did, and by making 'reality-testing' my predictions of disaster a habit, I became capable of slowing and even staving off my descent into nervous wreck territory.

Sandra had printed a sheet with a long and detailed list of questions I could turn to in the face of rising panic.

- Am I catastrophising or overestimating danger?
- What is the evidence that this thought is true? What is the evidence that it is not true?
- Have I confused a thought with a fact?
- What would I tell a friend if he/she had the same thought?
- What would a friend say about my thought?
- Am I 100 per cent sure that _____ will happen?
- How many times has _____ happened before?
- Is _____ so important that my future depends on it?
- What is the worst that could happen?
- If it did happen, what could I do to cope with or handle it?
- Is my judgement based on the way I feel instead of facts?
- Am I confusing 'possibility' with 'certainty'? It may be possible, but is it likely?
- Is this a hassle or a horror?

Being very explicit and rational about whatever sparked my feelings of foreboding was incredibly powerful, because it effectively starved my anxiety of what it thrived on: irrational fears.

With that sorted, the next giant leap in CBT is to create a new narrative.

Generate more positive thoughts

You are doing your best. You go to work every day that you feel well. Even with a chronic illness you have managed to obtain your degree and qualifications. You will be okay.

Once I identified the irrational predictions and negative distortions in my anxious thoughts, the idea was to replace them with new, healthier thoughts.

This involved casting my mind even further from the disaster it was habitually drawn to in search of something that is a rarity in the anxiety-riddled mind: a positive thought.

If on paper this appears entirely straightforward, let me say that, in theory, I agree. But in practice? It took time. When you are hardwired to doubt yourself, to automatically latch onto the familiar-if-distorted conclusions you have unknowingly gravitated towards for years, arresting the pattern is not as easy as it sounds.

Initially, even a tentative step into this territory felt anomalous. I was so self-conscious – even in the confines of my own head – that offering myself any positive feedback felt conceited. Scrutinising the landscape of my psychological make-up made me realise I'd been engaged in the business of embracing extreme 'either/or's right up until the point where my life crumbled around me.

I was either a lawyer with perfect attendance at work, or I was a total failure. I was either illness-free, or I was a total failure. I was either capable of withstanding the pressure of life every single day without a moment of weakness, or I was a total failure. I was either dressed immaculately, or I was a total failure. There was no nuance, which, in the inevitably nuanced realm of human life, was a problem.

The liberating truth I extracted from rehab was that I was – and remain – a human being. I have a chronic illness and suffer from anxiety, but that is neither the end nor the beginning of it. I was – and am – many other things, some of which are terrific, some of which aren't. I'm kind and considerate, hard-working and loyal. I am also sensitive and stubborn and tend to ruminate on all manner of things I shouldn't. In every single endeavour I undertake, all of these characteristics will come along with me. Sometimes they will help me succeed and sometimes they will cause me to fail.

Accepting that, and recognising the plague of perfectionism, was more than half of my battle. It explained to me why it felt like things never got easier. It explained why no matter how hard I tried or how many boxes I ticked, I never felt the joy of doing enough or being enough.

The idea that there was another way to live, that could eliminate fear, was exhilarating.

Theodore Roosevelt was right
(comparison is the thief of joy)

September 2007

Sandra's room was becoming so familiar that it almost felt like my own living room. It was carpeted, and her desk in the back corner was the only hint it was an office. Sandra always sat in an upholstered wing armchair while I adopted the righthand side of the small sofa opposite. We each had a small console table beside us: mine with tissues and water, hers with notepaper, pens and her compact glasses holder.

'Georgie, from what you have told me I don't think bullying would be too harsh a description for some of the behaviour you have described from that first boss.'

'No, I wouldn't say that. I think the thing is I am quite sensitive and so I didn't really respond very well with yelling and intense pressure.'

'Is yelling something you think some people *are* comfortable with at work?'

'Well, I mean, there are lots of people who *do* cope with it. Lots of people don't even seem to be impacted by it. I'm not one of them, but that's my fault. Plenty of people survive in stressful work environments.'

'Right.'

It's a credit to Sandra's tact that she didn't straight out ask how the whole clinging to a job I hated was working out for me. While I wasn't exactly eager to return to corporate law, quitting still felt too scary to seriously contemplate.

The elephant in this spacious Gold Coast room was that I was sitting in a psychiatric facility and yet I still found it hard to say that, perhaps, at this point in time, a large commercial law firm wasn't where I wanted to be.

'I just don't see why it should be so much harder for me than other people,' I said. 'I think it's a cop-out if I resign while other people are very capable of sticking it out?'

Sandra sighed, rearranged her glasses and raised her eyebrows.

It's easy, now, to gloss over the fact that deciding corporate law wasn't for me was akin to wresting teeth from my jaw. Despite the fact it should have been blindingly obvious, it was bloody tough. Even in rehab.

Over the past year, Mum, Dad and Nick had ventured the suggestion that I resign, multiple times, individually and collectively, but I had stonewalled them every time. I had studied law, done clerkships, secured a job, completed a graduate program, been admitted as a solicitor and now I was going to walk away? Into what? I had no backup plan.

My sessions with this diminutive woman, who had the power

to get through to me with just a change in expression, helped to tease out small cracks in that paradigm – and if that sounds simple, it wasn't.

Had I been sneaking out of the law office to see a psychologist during lunchtime, I doubt I would have been very receptive to these suggestions. But with Sandra, in hospital, I was. A raised eyebrow from Sandra was enough to make me consider whether I might be exercising some twisted 'logic' to justify remaining in a job I didn't like.

Maybe, regardless of the fact that I am sensitive and have Crohn's disease, getting yelled at isn't healthy or helpful? Maybe it's bullying? Maybe it's not surprising that it was difficult? Even if it wasn't bullying, does it matter? Maybe the fact others could have coped better with it is irrelevant? If I can't cope, what else matters?

'The thing is, when I was at the office, it felt like I was having an affair,' I said. 'Not because people *were* having affairs, but because I felt like my heart was somewhere else. I didn't want to be there. I didn't belong. And I hated that I felt like that.'

'That level of dissonance is hard to ignore, but you are almost squirming admitting it. Why do you think there is so much tension around that intuition?'

'Honestly? I don't know. I feel guilty and ashamed for not wanting to be there. For not liking it. In my most recent rotations I worked under people who I genuinely liked and admired and respected, but I didn't race into work thinking I wanted their jobs. I really didn't want to be there.'

'Why does saying that make you uncomfortable?'

'Because who am I to judge them? To dislike their careers? They are successful men and women and I'm five seconds out of university and think I know better than they do?'

'It's interesting because all of the words you use and your body language make it very clear that working in a big commercial firm isn't what you like or enjoy, but you are quite determined to persevere,' Sandra said. 'It would be one thing to love being a physiotherapist, for example, but to develop RSI so severe that the vocation became almost untenable. There is tension in that scenario – quite literally – because there is a pull between the dream and the reality. You don't even have the dream, but you don't want to let it go. Why?'

'I have wondered that, and I guess all I keep thinking is that maybe I don't like it because I'm weak, or I'm not as smart or hard-working as other lawyers are. Isn't it indulgent to quit a job just because it's not easy?'

'This is that same theme again, Georgie. You are holding yourself hostage to imagined standards. You are punishing yourself for not living up to "other people",' Sandra said, using her fingers to make quotation marks.

'Other people' didn't flinch when they were yelled at. They always knew the right thing to say and the right documents to attach to the right emails. They actually understood the Corporations Act instead of merely pretending to. They dressed perfectly. They were never late. They were never sick and they certainly didn't ever cry in the bathrooms at work. Actually, they probably never cried anywhere. They were not heartsink patients. They would be able to survive surgery and still go a round in a boxing ring. 'Other people' were not weak. They didn't quit their job just because they didn't love it.

Until that moment, I hadn't been consciously aware of the existence of these imaginary friends, nor how influential they were. 'Other people', a group of obnoxiously judgemental characters I imagined watching my every move, didn't exist. Some people land themselves in psychological distress on account of actually having difficult-to-please, ultra-judgemental parents who make their existence quite suffocating. Not me. I was blessed with the least judgemental parents around, so I appointed a crew of unreasonable characters to act the part: I let them sit on my shoulders and shout me into misery day in, day out like a harsh parent might.

Why?

In part because I hadn't quite grasped the idea of there being anything valuable about me unless it hit a mark on some kind of externally validating yardstick, like a 'good' job. I had not contemplated – and I cannot tell you how much I wish I was exaggerating here – that doing what I wanted was not only a possibility, but a legitimate and sensible option.

Another enduring lesson I extracted from rehab was that when I did compare myself to others, I never came out on top. In the echo chamber of my mind, my frequent attempts at comparison simply served to reveal a catalogue of my own flaws and shortcomings: I was not as smart or loved or pretty or successful or happy or fun or popular as anyone else. This, coupled with my proclivity for perfectionism, was a perfect storm. They fed off one another

To thwart it, I had to build some self-esteem, but I also had to recognise that engaging in constant comparison was in itself toxic and futile.

Who am I trying to kid? What does it matter if I'm not the smartest or most successful person? Who's ranking me? What am I trying to prove?

When we were having this conversation, I was, in conventional terms, the most unsuccessful I had ever been. I don't think I had ever 'failed' as comprehensively before, and yet I felt less like a failure than usual. My mind wasn't preoccupied, as it usually was, with assessing my own state against others'. Despairing over the gap between my own perceived inadequacies and the infinite qualities I projected onto everyone else just seemed unnecessary. The only plausible explanation I can offer for this change is that being scared of never being well again shifted my paradigm.

I started to recognise that this was my life, that it was my mistakes and my flaws and my illnesses that had landed me in hospital, and the fact other people had not succumbed to the same forces was neither here nor there. I wasn't in a race with anyone except myself. And to be honest, I didn't want to run anyway. I just wanted to stop and live.

Constantly comparing myself to others had paralysed me. The fear of falling short was a powerful force that kept me in a job I hated. It stopped me from taking my health seriously. It stopped me from doing anything that I feared would confirm that compared to everyone else I was deeply inadequate.

At the risk of inducing nausea, the only way I could avoid needlessly making joy-sucking comparisons was to accept who I was and where I was. I wouldn't overcome the comparison trap by starting to believe that I was better than other people – I couldn't convince myself of that if I tried. But my circumstances, quite fortuitously, forced me to accept that I was who I was, flaws and all, and that what other people were or weren't doing was not relevant.

With every day and session that passed, it became clear that a number of interconnected issues had helped conspire against my sound mind and health. The perfect storm of my undoing was either contributed to, accelerated by or not helped by the fact I had anxiety, and that I was a perfectionist with low self-esteem and a penchant for distorted, problematic thinking. I was also physically unwell and had categorically ignored my wellbeing.

These were exciting developments insofar as I was beginning to understand that these problems could be overcome *and* I was being taught how to do that.

~

Throughout those two weeks, it seemed my life was transforming from the inside out, but there was still a spanner to be thrown into the works of my rehab stint.

It happened in the head psychiatrist's office, as I was proudly describing the improvement in my health.

'I have done the walks almost every afternoon, I'm really enjoying the work with Sandra and I *feel* good. I'm sleeping, I like going to bed and waking up. It's actually hard to believe the difference.'

'It's terrific that you are feeling so much better,' he said. 'From all reports you have really thrown yourself into the program, which has obviously helped enormously.'

He then paused and I could sense something was coming. 'There is one issue I wanted to raise, though,' he said.

I felt my heart begin to beat a little faster.

'I would caution you away from believing that stress or anxiety has caused your vertigo,' he said.

My eyes stung. Shame and fear rose in my throat. Was I stupid for believing it so wholeheartedly? 'Then what do you think *has* caused my dizziness then?'

'I don't have a definitive diagnosis for you. Stress and anxiety can certainly have a physiological impact on the body, but I am personally not convinced that it works in the way you seem to believe.'

The rug was torn out from underneath me. Believing that stress had precipitated my breakdown had been my circuit breaker: it was the reason I was admitted to hospital, put on medication, and the reason that, for the first time in months, I had started to entertain the idea I might recover. Whether it was the root cause or not, the stress theory was the salvation I had been desperately searching for. It was an answer that made sense to me, and even though, deep down, I still genuinely believed it, the psychiatrist's words reopened the abyss of fear and the unknown.

'It doesn't change the good work you have done here, Georgie.'

He knew I was upset, but I didn't have a fight in me. I nodded, walked back to my room, sat on my bed and sobbed.

'G, talk to me. What's happened?' Mum's voice was panicked on the other end of the line. 'Darling?'

'He, he … doesn't believe the vertigo is from anxiety,' I eventually got out, my chest heaving.

'Who, darling? Take a deep breath. Just breathe. It's okay.'

'It's not okay, Mum. Of course it's not okay. He thinks something else is causing the vertigo, so what's even the point in me being here?'

'*Who?*'

'The psychiatrist!'

'But remember what Dr Wagner said?'

'Yes, of course I remember what Dr Wagner said!' My fear had turned to fury. 'That's the whole reason I'm here, but if the head of this bloody hospital – who has spent his whole stupid career working with mental illness – says mental illness couldn't have caused my vertigo, why would I not listen? *Why?* There's obviously something else wrong.'

The line was silent. I could hear Mum sigh, but I may as well have heard her heart break.

'Can I call you back a bit later?' Her voice broke, and I hated myself.

Why did I have to be so awful to her? Why did I have to unchain my terror on her? It was unfair; I knew that. It scared me to think I had pushed her to the point where she couldn't help.

'Of course,' I said, hanging up.

When Sue walked in I was still on my bed with my phone in my hand. I looked up, and when I met her eyes I started crying again.

'What happened?' she asked with genuine surprise, walking over to my side of our room. 'You were so happy when you left …'

I was, and realising that made me even sadder.

'I am awful and I have broken my mum.'

Sue wrapped her arms around me.

'Hey, your mum loves you. You know that,' she said. 'This is hard for you both.'

She sat next to me while I told her what the psychiatrist had said.

'Sue, I cannot even think about there being some weird explanation for my vertigo that no one can find,' I said. 'I just can't. It means I'll never get better. I can't be dizzy forever.'

'You won't be. It is going to pass.'

That afternoon, fear and guilt festered. I called Nick and cried: it was an unwelcome return to the style of conversation we had become accustomed to. Me sobbing, him soothing.

'I just don't know why he would even say that to you,' he said.

'The thing you have to try and remember is that you're already feeling better.'

'I know that, but I do still feel a bit dizzy at times and I do feel weak,' I said. 'I don't feel 100 per cent.'

'It took you months to get into this place and it's going to take you more than ten days to get back to feeling normal.'

'Even if I do, Mum hates me. With good reason.'

'I'll call her. You know how hard this is. She wants you to feel better almost more than you do,' he said. 'You're scared.'

'I know.'

I didn't go for the walk that day, like I had been in the habit of doing, and I barely spoke at dinner. One drop of doubt was enough to plunge me back into darkness.

I didn't recognise it at the time, but this conflict was – strangely – the ultimate test I faced in rehab, and somehow I found it within myself to accept what felt right to me.

I pushed aside the temptation to talk myself down, to catastrophise, to take on the words of one important and qualified person as gospel. For the first time in my adult life, I offered myself an olive branch and listened to my instincts.

Everything I had heard and learned during my stay had reinforced my understanding that stress and anxiety were major issues for me. I had come to accept, as kind Dr Wagner pointed out, that stress could have a physical impact on the body, and I couldn't dismiss the possibility that I had worried myself sick. Backing myself felt foreign and unfamiliar and took more than a kernel of courage, but it also felt unbelievably good.

The next morning, after breakfast and before group therapy, I called Mum and apologised. She accepted. Of course, she did. But I knew I had pushed her too far and I promised myself I would refrain from doing it again. She could not be my punching bag, any more than I could be.

Part Three

Better

There is another way

September 2007

'Hi, James. It's Georgie Dent. Can you please call me back when you get a chance?'

Butterflies fluttered in my stomach as I sat on the steps of Mum and Dad's back deck, the sun streaming onto my legs. It was the Monday after I had finished my stint in rehab: my first day back in the real world. After psyching myself up and painstakingly plugging in the numbers on the handset, I had reached my boss's voicemail. Thirty seconds later, my mobile pinged with a text.

Just in a meeting. I'll call you back in five. James.

I decided to wait outside in the sun. I was nervous but not scared. It had become crystal clear to me that working in corporate law was not what I needed, nor what I wanted. I hadn't been there for over four months, so the call was mostly symbolic, but I was about to formally resign. Sitting still, enjoying the sun, being idle, felt heady; it was a kind of peace I had only just gotten a taste of. Eventually my ringtone interrupted the quiet.

'Hello, Georgie speaking,' I answered.

'Georgie!' James' voice boomed through the line. 'How are you?'

'I'm pretty good thanks, James.'

'We miss you. Are you all better yet? When are you coming back?'

'Actually, that's the reason for my call,' I said. 'I've spent the past fortnight in a psychiatric hospital and I've decided that the best thing for me, and particularly my health, is to resign. The only thing that really matters right now is getting myself better.'

'Mate, I'm so sorry. You really have had such a rough time,' he said. 'We've all been hoping you were going to come back, but really we all just want you to get better.'

I was honest about where I'd been, what I'd experienced, and I was resolute that my health – physical and mental – was my only priority. Being totally honest felt good too: I wasn't hiding from the truth, nor pretending things were better or different than they were, as I'd always done in the past. And rather than feeling embarrassed or ashamed, I felt proud. I had experienced something awful, I'd realised that mental illness was a live concern for me and I was taking steps to protect myself from that happening again.

If James was shocked by my admissions he didn't let on. His kindness was humbling.

'Thank you, James. I really appreciate your understanding.'

'Will you come in so we can give you a little farewell?'

'Of course. When I'm back in Sydney I'll get in touch and we can arrange a time.'

No other phone call I have made – either before or after that day – has felt as profound and trivial as that conversation did.

It was huge and it was tiny. It meant everything and it meant nothing.

The fact I had worked hard for so many years to land the job didn't matter. The fact it was a 'good' job didn't matter. The fact I had no backup job, nor backup plan, didn't matter. Nothing mattered except the newfound appreciation that my health was the most precious commodity I had.

I called Nick immediately afterwards, bemused by the enormity of the choice I had just made, which took nothing less than a breakdown to reach, and just minutes to effect.

'I'm free! I did it! I really did it!'

'You did it?!' he asked with happy shock. 'What did James say?'

'He was lovely. He said he was sad but he understood. I can't believe it's done.'

'I can't either. Darling, I'm so happy for you.'

I sat on the steps grinning like a Cheshire cat. I knew I could no longer maintain the stress levels I had previously accepted. Working as a lawyer absolutely did not cause my breakdown: it could have happened in any field. *I* caused my breakdown, but being in a genuinely stressful workplace accelerated my demise. Some people can withstand working around the clock, a boss with unchecked anger issues, and the pressure of clients and billable units without physically absorbing stress, but I couldn't. Not sustainably. Not in a way that was compatible with the 'meaningful life' I had begun to picture for myself.

I didn't want to spend my days racing to the bathroom, fuelled by dread and adrenaline. I was tired of that. I liked breathing. I liked not feeling panicked. I liked feeling that merely existing didn't need to be a battle. To make that happen I had to manage stress, and leaving corporate law was a big first step.

I checked out of rehab a very different person than I'd been when I entered it, and the fact that sounds woefully clichéd doesn't render it any less true. After months feeling trapped outside of life, unsure independence was a blessing I'd ever enjoy again, the idea of being able to step back in and participate in life at all was intoxicating, let alone participating in life on my own terms.

I felt like a different person living in a brand-new world that I had only begun to see. The limits and grievances and jeers that I had heaped on myself, day in, day out for more than a decade, were revealed as needless and optional. It had dawned on me that there was another way to live, an easier way to live, and I was ready to start trying it.

I moved back to Sydney and gradually eased myself back into life. My GP was brought up to speed and, as decided when I left rehab, I was booked in to continue CBT with a new psychologist. In a welcome stroke of luck, some relatives of mine needed someone to housesit their place for a month, so Nick and I put our hands up and happily began cohabiting again. Nick was at the tail end of his commuting between Sydney and Canberra, as the rugby season was winding down, and we set up a new version of normal.

But I needed a job. Another relative of mine, who owned a retail business, arranged an interview for a casual job selling clothes at David Jones, which gave me a perfect low-key return to the workforce. I started out doing a couple of shifts a week, five hours at a time, and I loved it. Having a role to punctuate my time was welcome: not because I *had* to do something, but because I could. It felt good to be useful.

Depending on the time of my shift, my days varied. I would usually wake up around 7am and go for a half-hour walk around the neighbourhood before having breakfast. I loved the feeling of having a shower after *doing* something: using my body. Once dressed I'd jump on a bus to the city from around the corner and relish the commute. Being an active participant in the world again felt almost illicit. I'd disembark the bus a few hundred metres from David Jones, where I'd happily make my way to the staff entrance.

In any given shift, my time would be split between helping customers find something on the shop floor, folding items so the displays were neat, steaming various garments and going to the stockroom downstairs to help sort new deliveries. All the tasks were so practical that I found the work legitimately rewarding. On my break I'd sit down somewhere with a coffee or my favourite yoghurt and a book.

Taking a job in retail for the sake of my health was something I couldn't have done before I fell to pieces; my ego wouldn't have countenanced it. And yet it was the best decision I could have made because it allowed me to gradually make my way back into the world of work.

I swam regularly, joined a yoga studio and relished every second of being physically active. It was gently, gently, but the days felt highly charged. For at least a year the world had been in greyscale, and suddenly it was brilliant, vibrant and colourful.

As my balance returned and I felt stronger, I could do more physically, and the high these activities elicited was extraordinary. There was gratitude that I was able to do these things – to luxuriate in the water while my body glided through the pool, to feel my muscles strengthen after languishing disused for so long. But there was also the mental sensation, the elation, it delivered afterwards. The thrill of being alive was never as vivid to me as it was during the glorious days where my time was spent working my retail shifts and exercising. Not obsessively. Not to punish myself. Not to lose weight, flatten my stomach or tone my arms, but to revel in moving my body because I could and because it felt good.

The link between physical movement and mood is well documented. There is barely a situation where exercise won't improve a person's mental landscape to some extent. It might not wholly resolve a manifestation of mental illness, deliver a solution to a tricky work situation, put a marriage back together or 'fix' whatever is causing trouble, but it will rarely make things worse. It is more likely to bring clarity of mind, an improved mood and better sleep – an arsenal of benefits that will only help a person face whichever lemon life is throwing at them.

In the realm of mental illness, these benefits are exponential. The improvements in mood are thought to be caused by the increase in blood circulation to the brain, an influence on the hypothalamic-pituitary-adrenal (HPA) axis – the central stress response system – and your physical capacity to respond to stress. Some researchers say exercise is undervalued as an intervention in mental illness.

It was certainly invaluable to my rebuilding. Session by session, I cleared my mind, I focused on my breath and let myself savour the movement. While swimming laps or pounding a pavement, it was far harder to succumb to the foetal position I had habitually favoured when contemplating fears and doubts. Exercise gave me time to process thoughts with clarity, without succumbing to the angst, so I started saving my 'worries' for when I was walking. Or swimming. Along the way, I got stronger and fitter, and gradually my new habit delivered peace of mind.

If humankind has a wonder drug at its disposal, exercise is it, and it's unrivalled. Moving can help make everyone feel better and especially those feeling burnt out or run down or impacted by mental illness. It's why I find walking into a chemist and seeing the vast array of expensive products for various outcomes – better circulation, weight loss, decreased blood pressure, improved sleep – so baffling. Exercise is proven to do all of that and more, free of charge. No bottle! No tablet! No cost!

Embracing exercise was undoubtedly one of the more tangible changes I made to my daily existence post-breakdown, but it was only one component of my progression from an individual who approached my own wellbeing like a masochist to someone a little smarter and a lot kinder.

I could not live a life in which relaxation and exercise were optional extras, luxuries I could tack on to the end of each week, or month, or holiday, or whenever an opportunity presented. Being well had to be a daily reality, and it was up to me to establish habits to achieve that. I had to build a life in which taking care of myself was embedded and intentional, and that was more of a paradigm shift than a subtle tweak.

In pursuing feeling good, for once I was creating a legitimately fulfilling cycle. The more things I did that made me feel good, the better I felt and the more inclined I was to do more things that made me feel good. If I could have bottled the clarity of that understanding into little tonic and sold it the world over, I would be a very rich woman, and the planet would be filled with citizens diligently pursuing their wellbeing.

I had been back in Sydney for almost two months when I realised that, miracle of miracles, my Crohn's disease had abated. The symptoms that had dogged me daily for the past eight years literally vanished, and the realisation that it had been days, and then weeks, without so much as a hiccup, stopped me in my tracks. *I could eat without fear! I could live without feeling sick!* My days were no longer marked by the painful stomach spasms I couldn't remember not enduring. Life without debilitating depression and chronic anxiety was one wonderful thing, but life without the ghastly physical effects of Crohn's was another totally magical thing altogether. It seemed too good to be true.

'So there's something I've been avoiding saying out loud because I haven't wanted to jinx it, but I can't keep it a secret anymore,' I blurted out one night while Nick and I were on the couch watching TV.

'Hmmm?' he said with a mixture of interest and unease.

'My tummy is totally fine. I haven't had a cramp or pain or anything revolting for weeks. I can't remember it ever feeling so normal. It's like it just finally learned to work!'

'I had wondered about that,' he said with a grin. 'You haven't mentioned any problems for weeks. I wonder whether the medications have helped settle it?'

Because this was before smart-phones, I waited until the next day when I was at my laptop to investigate the mysterious disappearance of my symptoms. Google led me to discover that one of the medications I had been prescribed for the vertigo had been used with some success on Crohn's disease patients in Canada.

A decade on, to my ongoing disbelief, my Crohn's symptoms have never returned. If there was ever any tangible proof that I had worried myself sick, it was the potent fact I started to feel healthier than I ever had, and conquered a longstanding chronic illness, almost as soon as I got my anxiety under control was potent.

To this day, I remain on the medications I was prescribed in rehab. Obviously, I'm not a doctor or a health practitioner, so I am not remotely qualified to comment on the science of it all, but there is a recognised relationship between anxiety, inflammation and autoimmune conditions. Exactly how it works isn't known but it seems unlikely, to this layperson at least, that these three things could be wreaking havoc simultaneously in one body without there being some link between them. The fact that all three simultaneously receded reinforces it.

I spent the remaining three months of 2007 working in David Jones, seeing Miriam, a psychologist who I came to adore, looking after myself and taking each day as it came. The version of me who had started the year – who considered anything less than a twelve-hour day at the office deficient – would not have recognised who I had become, but I was content in a way I had never been.

Still, there were hiccups. A few weeks into my transition back to Sydney, I came down with a pretty decent head cold that totally threw me. I had become so sensitive and attuned to how I felt – and mostly how I felt was good – that waking up feeling like a truck had run over my head was frightening. Before I knew it I was catastrophising about how I would probably feel sick forever, that this cold was proof again of my deficiencies, that I probably couldn't handle even a casual retail job because my constitution was weak.

My weekly CBT session with Miriam helped arrest my descent into despair, as did the fact I recovered from the head cold within a few days.

But it still wasn't over. A few weeks later, I arrived for my CBT appointment in quite a state. Nick and I had been housesitting for some of my relatives while they were overseas, and the only task we'd been given for the privilege of occupying their lovely home was keeping the plants watered. Nick had been away for a few nights, and I had come home from work one afternoon to find that several of the plants had wilted badly. I was wracked with panic. The second I sat down and confessed to Miriam what I had done, I burst into tears.

'I had one job and I couldn't even do that. They trusted me to housesit and I have let them down so badly,' I cried. 'I killed all the plants. I am irresponsible and useless.'

These were the actual thoughts I had, and the feeling they triggered was unqualified shame. It was the first time since leaving rehab that I had felt truly riddled with the guilt and distress that I had long been accustomed to. I was clearly entering troubled territory, so Miriam got to work with me breaking it down through this CBT prism:

Event → Thoughts → Reactions

Event: Some plants wilted in the sun while I was at work.
Thoughts: This is because I am useless.
Reaction: Feel worthless, ashamed and cry.

Miriam asked me to consider the 'whole picture'. The truth was it had been super dry, it hadn't rained in over a month, and I had been watering the plants regularly. Nick and I had missed the watering on two days when it happened to be particularly hot, and some plants had wilted.

Was the state of the plants the whole sum of my being? Had I burnt down the house or hosted a party or wrecked the furniture? Was I really irresponsible? Was it possible that even if

I had watered the plants that morning, they might have wilted anyway? Was I going to try to sort it out?

At the end of that session I felt lighter. The world wasn't going to cave in because a few plants wilted. It was not proof I was a hopeless individual with no redeeming features. It was something that happened that I was going to fix.

In my case, embarking on CBT was immediately useful because of situations precisely like this: it gave me a practical solution to my problem. Doing CBT isn't a set-and-forget exercise, but people often derive benefit from it within a relatively short period of time. It's a toolkit to run a mental detox: it helps me refrain from force-feeding myself a steady diet of undesirable, unhelpful and unnecessary worries.

Sometimes I would forget that the way I thought was a choice. There were occasions when all I could see was a great big list of my own failures, where I saw everything that went 'wrong' as a product of my own shortcomings. Where I couldn't help but imagine all of the things that would go wrong. Where even the smallest molehills became mountains. I still fall into this trap, regularly.

Whenever I enter this particular den of despair, I must search for a way out. Sometimes I have done this by seeing a psychologist, and other times I have managed it by myself, diligently engaging in the CBT techniques I was taught. I have to unpack the story I'm telling myself, test out alternatives and focus my mental energy elsewhere. It is a perpetual work in progress.

As I worked through my post-breakdown checklist, I inadvertently edged closer to something I had steadfastly avoided for most of my life: being myself, like, my *actual* self.

Gradually, as I stripped back layer after layer of the facade I had erected in a bid to secure the approval of others, I happened upon a more authentic version of myself – and, yes, that is one of the more gag-inducing sentences I've ever written. But it's true.

I had been holding myself hostage to all sorts of rubbish that had, in myriad ways, conspired to hide who I actually was. Letting go of that was liberating.

After I fell apart, it was suddenly apparent that anyone whose approval of me relied on my remaining some kind of perfectly functioning robot – a perfect student, a perfect lawyer, a perfect anything – was entirely superfluous. It was also clear the only person who had ever expected that from me, was me.

'Being me' didn't entail a dramatic makeover: from the outside there was no grand transformation, but from the inside it was revolutionary. I began by letting myself be guided by what worked for me. What I wanted and what I needed became my absolute priorities, and it meant being truly self-centred, which I relished.

As our housesitting stint drew to a close in October, Nick and I began thinking about our living arrangements. He had signed a contract with an ACT-based rugby team for the following year that would require him to spend half his time in Canberra, so I wasn't keen on renting a place by ourselves. I wasn't sure what 2008 would bring, but I was hoping I'd be ready to dip my toe back into the world of full-time work, and I didn't want to be alone for half the week. Rather than pretend otherwise, I said so, and we set about finding a share house. It wasn't exactly the done thing – we were both 'supposed' to be moving away from our share house university days – but it was what we both wanted, and it worked a treat. We moved into an incredibly social house in the eastern suburbs and made a lifelong friend from the arrangement.

It was a little decision that represented a marked departure from my modus operandi. I began to live a lot more honestly and a little more bravely. I didn't have to do the 'done' thing. I could do what felt right for me.

Living the dream

February 2008

I was standing on a bus packed with commuters flocking to the eastern suburbs, feeling hot and sticky after an eight-hour shift selling clothes. It was late afternoon but not quite peak hour, and I had been contemplating whether I should duck to Bondi for a dip. Suddenly, I noticed I felt irritated at the cramped space, the lack of air, and the fact the bus had come ten minutes late. I hadn't experienced this type of everyday annoyance since my return to life.

Alfonso, my friend from the law firm, had warned me this would happen. When he was at uni he'd been diagnosed with a brain tumour halfway through his degree that required surgery, and he'd spent six months of being virtually bed-ridden. He and I spoke regularly while I was unwell, and he told me, more than once, that when I got better life would feel better than I had ever remembered. He described the high experienced after being able to live again as a joy that almost made the ordeal worth it, but he warned that it would eventually wear off. There would come a time, he promised, when I found myself irritated by something truly trivial – a bus running late, a parking ticket, a rude shop assistant – and the rose-tinted lenses of my recovery would clear.

He was right. It was a bus that did it! I almost laughed as I realised it and I reached for my phone to send him a text letting him know. As soon as I did, I saw a notification that I had missed a call from another friend, Austin. He'd left a voicemail message.

'Hey G. Hope you're well. I know you are looking into work options and I've just seen that *BRW Magazine* is recruiting researchers. The ad says they want students or recent graduates with a business degree and it made me think of you. You should check it out. I've sent you an email with the link. Talk soon.'

My irritation no longer mattered and the idea of a swim at the beach was shelved that very second. I wanted to know everything, but as this was in the prehistoric days before mobile internet was common, I had to get home to investigate further. Fifty minutes later, having stepped into a cold shower to wash away the day's grime, I grabbed my laptop and set up at the kitchen table.

Fairfax Media was looking to recruit between six and eight researchers for *BRW Magazine* on fixed three-month contracts, compiling the data around the annual 'Rich 200 List', listing the wealthiest men and women in the country. There was a line in the ad stating that the role would include 'working closely alongside reporters', which was enough for my heart to almost stop beating.

The ad said the roles would be ideal for candidates with a degree in business or commerce and encouraged final-year business students and recent graduates to consider applying. I very legitimately ticked all of the selection criteria, so I spent the next two hours giddily compiling my resume and a cover letter. Before it was even dark, I had submitted an application, and my imagination was running wild at the prospect of working inside a media organisation.

For almost a month I had felt ready, physically and emotionally, to commit to full-time work again, and in my mind I had cast the net wide for options. By this stage I was still seeing Miriam weekly, but she was happy enough with my progress that we were going to start spreading my appointments out to fortnightly and then monthly.

I wasn't convinced that I couldn't have a career in law, though I had decided a big firm wasn't going to work, so I looked into all manner of different positions. I looked into government roles, policy positions and small law firms, and tried to keep an open mind about what I might actually enjoy doing. Quite early in my search, a position for a junior lawyer at the ABC had caught my eye.

In my heart of hearts, I still wanted to be a journalist, so this job seemed a fitting marriage of my skills *and* interests. I spent a few nights putting an application together, during which time I realised it was a long shot. Miraculously, when I learned I wasn't successful in even securing an interview, it did not rattle me. I simply accepted that I didn't have the requisite years of experience and moved on, and my lord, let me tell you, this angst-free development was delicious.

I effectively chose to bypass the existential crisis this type of rejection would ordinarily have triggered, because I recognised it wasn't a big deal. Me! Not falling apart at rejection! Having perspective! Lying in a ditch refusing to move for half an hour while someone you love begs you to get up is bad. Not getting an interview? Less calamitous.

But the letter of rejection from the ABC did prompt me to sit down and consider what I wanted to do more carefully. Not what I 'should' do, nor what I thought would look good on my resume, but what I actually *wanted* to do, and all roads led to journalism.

A few days after submitting my application to *BRW* I received a phone call from the 'Rich List' editor, John, asking me to come in for an interview the following week. I was thrilled, and even happier after the interview was done. It was informal, but we covered lots of ground and John said he thought I was particularly well qualified for the role.

I drove away from Pyrmont with a good feeling that the job would be mine.

When I found out I was right, I was working in the city. I was expecting the call, but we weren't allowed our phones on the shop floor. The hours of a shift had never felt so long as they did on that Friday. I raced to the staff locker room as soon as my manager sent me on a break and was overjoyed to see I had a missed call and a voicemail message from John. I literally jumped with joy when I played it back. The thrill of landing this job after the year I'd had was profound.

A few weeks later, the role commenced, and from the minute I arrived I knew I had found my calling. On the first day, Sean, the editor-in-chief, who had only just started on the magazine himself, walked over to the desks where all the researchers sat and offered to take us out for coffee.

Instinctively, I stood up. 'Oh, I'll run down now and order everyone's coffees if you'd like?'

He looked at me like I was a little mad and laughed. 'Or we could all go down together, and *I* can order the coffees?'

It felt so odd and egalitarian, and it took me a little while to realise the hierarchical style of a law firm, to which I was accustomed, wasn't universal.

Over coffee, Sean asked each of us about what we were doing, why we'd applied and what we were hoping to get out of the experience. When it was my turn to answer, I left out the bit about having just had a total breakdown, but said I was a qualified solicitor looking to make a career change. Journalism had always been my dream, but after being at uni the structure of law had lured me in that direction.

Two weeks later, Sean called me over and asked if I'd be willing to write a short piece for the magazine on the latest immigration figures. I couldn't agree fast enough and set about tackling the task. Writing 350 words from a bunch of facts and figures was a challenge I enjoyed, and I was proud of what I submitted.

'Georgie,' Sean called out later that afternoon as he wove through the pod of desks where I sat. 'Let's have a chat.'

I practically ran to his desk.

'Were you serious when you said you were interested in a career in journalism?'

'Very,' I said. 'That's why I applied in the first place.'

'And what have you made of it so far?'

'It's better than I'd imagined.'

He laughed. 'There is no better job in the world than being a reporter.'

That was my assessment too, having spent a few weeks sandwiched between two reporters, listening intently to everything they said.

'You did a good job with that piece this morning. The thing is, I want us to increase the magazine's coverage of the legal sector, and my thinking is that if you worked for a big law firm you are probably very capable of writing about that,' he said. 'We can teach you the journalism side of things, and I'm going to assume that because of your legal training you'll learn the ropes quickly.'

He set me a few more writing tasks before he organised an interview with the editor of the *Financial Review*. The next week, Sean dropped an envelope on my desk: it was a contract to begin working as a trainee reporter as soon as the research term was completed.

I could not believe my luck. For a long time, whenever I explained the story of how I moved from law into media, I said the universe had rewarded me. That I got lucky because of what I had endured. It was only much more recently that I began to consider that perhaps I had helped make that luck. That because I took on a research position with no guarantee of further employment and was willing to test out one of my dreams, I put myself in a position where that dream was in reach.

In the decade I have worked as a journalist, there have been stressful days, frustrations, mistakes and challenges. Plenty of them. But with my hand on my heart, I can say there has never been a single moment when I have doubted my vocation. Since my very first day as a proper reporter, I felt like I was doing what I was meant to be doing. Being able to ask questions suited my curious nature, writing felt natural and my days were charged with a genuine sense of purpose. I wasn't changing the world in the work I was doing, but by doing work that I wanted to do, I changed *my* world.

Since changing careers, I have never experienced anything like the dissonance I felt daily as a lawyer, and in hindsight it was the chasm between my head and my heart that made life as a junior lawyer toxic for me. Given my health, the long hours and stressful culture of a big corporate firm weren't ideal, but had I been engaged and passionate about the work, I am not sure it would have ended the way it did.

'Do what you love' and 'follow your passion' are no doubt platitudes that aren't always practical. I get that, and I grappled with it often, but doing something that doesn't feel right isn't without its challenges either. I ruminated for a really long time about being trapped in a job I didn't like. Initially I punished myself for even indulging in such thoughts – was I really so entitled and spoiled that I thought I ought to like going to work every day?

I ignored it, I felt guilty because of it and I felt stuck. During the eighteen months I was living in my 'pinstriped prison', as author Lisa Pryor so aptly described young-professional life, my awareness of the various jobs around me was heightened.

I would sometimes walk from Nick's share house in Bondi Junction to my place in Darlinghurst before work, and along the way my eyes would dwell on everyone whose path I crossed. The baristas pouring coffee, florists unpacking their haul from the markets, personal trainers torturing their clients, men and women setting up their businesses, opening up real estate agencies, boutiques and cafes. How did they decide what job they wanted? Did they love their job or did they feel as trapped as I did? To my eye, they all looked so free, but this was undoubtedly a reflection of what I wanted to see. I wanted to believe it was possible to be free.

Being a legal reporter made me realise that I had been far from alone in feeling trapped in law. My role at *BRW* often involved interviewing big-firm partners, and in many instances my subjects had been informed by their media teams that I had worked at a big firm myself. It's not uncommon for legal reporters to have a background like mine, so it was hardly out of the ordinary, but I was surprised at how often my new career was met with curiosity rather than disdain.

Whenever I had an interview scheduled with a partner without a minder – either over the phone or in person – I came to anticipate a question that would nudge the door open on a discussion about life in a law firm.

Sometimes they were forthright and simply asked, 'How did you get out?' Other times it was subtler: 'You know, there was a time I thought about being a journalist/writer/lecturer/teacher,' they would say, before explaining the various ways in which life had intervened. How they got promoted or married or had children, and then, somehow, ten or fifteen or twenty years had passed and they were still in law.

It wouldn't be fair to say that every partner I interviewed expressed regret about their career choice, but enough did to make me realise I wasn't alone in harbouring my doubts. The number of partners who extended their sincere congratulations – even admiration – on account of me having 'made the jump', as it was so often described, was enlightening.

I had berated myself no end for feeling out of place in a big law firm. I was weighed down with guilt and angst for the duration of my stint because I didn't feel like it was the right place for me, but I was far from alone in feeling that way. These conversations inevitably reinforced an uncharacteristically positive thought I'd been road-testing: perhaps rather than being an indication of failure, my exit from law had been brave?

The fact I landed myself a job I loved was reward enough, but the fact it provided this perspective – this mirror into the minds of the bosses I had always wanted to interrogate – was an added blessing.

Adventure beckons

March 2009

By Autumn 2009 I was in a very good place. I was adoring my work: going to the office each day was a thrill, I felt well, physically and mentally, and for the first time Nick and I were both working full time. He had started as an intern at Wollongong Hospital in late January and was commuting back on weekends to the flat we shared with our friend Erin. Our life felt more 'ordinary', in the best sense of the word, than it ever had, but we knew that this moment of stability might be temporary.

One morning I was walking from the city to Pyrmont, making my way to Fairfax's offices, when our world changed yet again. There was not a cloud in the sky. Sydney Harbour was sparkling, the sun's reflection danced on the water and the flags lining either side of the pedestrian bridge over Darling Harbour waved gently. March had brought with it a hint of chill that meant I could walk to work without arriving in a layer of sweat. It was sublime. The contrast with my commute of old, in which bathroom stops were the vines I desperately swung between, couldn't have been starker.

It was around 8am when my mobile rang.

'I got in!' Nick's voice boomed through my little Nokia

handset. 'Oxford! They accepted me!'

'Oh my god!' I said with happy tears in my eyes. 'Congratulations!!'

'I can't believe it's happening!' he said.

'Me either!'

'What are you doing in September?' he asked.

I laughed. 'It depends.'

'Want to move to the UK?'

'I'll check my diary.'

I walked into work that Tuesday morning feeling elated. The year before, in early November, the week after Nick had graduated from medicine, he had been contacted by Oxford University and asked if he'd be interested in postgraduate study. He had unsuccessfully applied for a Rhodes scholarship to study there a few years earlier, and now he was being offered the chance to apply for a different course and a different scholarship, largely on account of his rugby credentials.

In his final year of medicine, during a prac placement at Sydney's St Vincent's Hospital in Darlinghurst, Nick had determined that he wanted to specialise in plastic and reconstructive surgery. A fourteen-hour operation in which a man had his throat and tongue reconstructed, using muscle from his hamstring after a cancerous growth had been excised, was what convinced Nick that this was the field he wanted to work in. Personally, I couldn't imagine anything worse, but to Nick this was a path with endless potential.

Speciality training programs, particularly in surgery, are highly competitive. After graduating from medicine, a doctor has to work in hospitals for two years: first as an intern and then as a resident. These positions are allocated by public hospitals and involve rotating between different wards and specialities, often involving at least a term or two in a country hospital. At the conclusion of those two years, doctors can then apply for senior resident or registrar positions with a view to getting into a training program of their choosing. The jobs are hard to get, the training positions harder still.

Before he even began his intern year, Nick made contact with a few plastic and reconstructive surgeons he'd met and asked for advice to help secure a position in the field down the track. Doing research and getting published in various medical journals, making his preference known to as many surgeons as possible and getting a Master's degree were among the steps he was advised to take.

By the end of November, he had submitted his application to do a Masters of Science at Oxford, but at the end of that process we'd both mentally put it to the side. There was no point planning for something we weren't sure would happen, and it seemed a long shot.

When he first got the call, we had both laughed at the ridiculousness of him canvassing a return to university when he had literally only just completed a six-year course over eight years, thanks to the time commitment of pursuing various rugby opportunities. Still, we were both giddy at having such a good excuse to live overseas. Travelling and living abroad was something we'd always talked about doing.

And the highs kept coming. A few weeks later, on Good Friday, during a walk at dusk on the farm he grew up on, Nick proposed and my heart exploded. Of course, I said yes. Later, as we shared the news with our families, happily gushing away about this exciting development, I thought back to my final attempt to push Nick away. It wasn't that long ago, really, but it felt like another life. Thank the lord above that Nick didn't listen to me.

Less than two years earlier, the idea that I'd be participating in a life that wasn't played out entirely on my parents' sofa had seemed far-fetched. That I was healthy, working in a job I adored, and had an overseas adventure beckoning was mind-blowing as it was. And now I was going to marry a man so extraordinary that I had no words to describe him, the man who had stood by my side when that could not have been less appealing. The love of my life.

The joy was exhilarating, and before the Easter weekend was over, we had decided to make our engagement a short one.

We were going to be based in the UK for a little under two years, the duration of Nick's course, so we decided to get married before we left Australia at the start of August. It was a whirlwind four months between April and August, organising the logistics of our relocation overseas and planning a wedding.

In the happy haze, it hadn't dawned on me that I was walking perilous ground in sacrificing the job of my dreams. We had long talked about living overseas together, and this seemed like the perfect reason to do it. Knowing, as I did, that we could survive less-than-sunny days filled me with confidence. It felt like we were embarking hand-in-hand on an exciting adventure, taking up an opportunity too good to pass up, together. That it was not *my* opportunity – at least not in a day-to-day sense – somehow escaped me.

In a catch-up with my boss Sean, earlier in the year, I had flagged the distant possibility of a move. Aside from being kind enough to give me the job I adored, he had turned out to be a wonderful manager – that rare type who brought out the very best in people without even trying. When he'd asked about my ambitions for the year ahead, I had told him this opportunity was on the horizon for Nick.

'You can't not do that!' he said without pause. 'You'd be mad to turn that sort of thing down, Georgie.'

'I know that. I really know that, but I love my job.'

'You'll sort yourself out a job over there. And what an adventure!'

Nonetheless, I cried while writing my resignation letter. Typing out those words reminded me of where I'd been and where I was now. I was leaving the job that had pulled me from the wreckage of a career and life in crisis, the job that had felt more right than anything I'd ever done, the job that buoyed me with the knowledge I could have a full and interesting career without sacrificing my health.

Still, there was more to life than work, and I knew that what Nick and I shared was among the things that meant more, so I handed the letter in without any sense that troubled times lay ahead.

~

'I'm going to give you a referral to see someone at Prince of Wales Private,' my Sydney GP said at the end of a general catch-up. 'She is a specialist obstetrician gynaecologist and will be able to give you a definitive answer about how a pregnancy might interact with your medication.'

'I mean, it's not something we want straight away, but I can only imagine that given my body's track record it will probably be tricky.' I laughed, rolling my eyes.

'The thing is, given you're going to be living away for a couple of years, you may as well have all the information now about what drugs you can and cannot take.'

At this appointment, I had confessed to my GP that towards the end of our two-year stint in the UK, Nick and I were open to starting a family. We had joked that flying home with a baby on board *in utero* would be amazing.

We visited the specialist together and were heartened when she advised that all of the medications I was on were safe during pregnancy. Those drugs were keeping everything working, and I was reluctant to give up any of them unnecessarily.

'From a medication perspective, you're certainly in the clear,' she said at the conclusion of the appointment. 'But, Georgie, given your history of endometriosis and the various medications you have taken for Crohn's over the years, conceiving might not happen overnight.'

'There is obviously no guarantee either way, but it might help to set out with the expectation that you won't fall pregnant quickly,' she said. 'You can save yourself some angst if you aren't expecting it immediately. Perhaps you could just be relaxed about contraception while you're away, and if it hasn't happened by your return, we can explore options. Good luck!'

Her advice seemed sensible and aligned with what Nick and I had both suspected.

~

The weekend after we finished up in our respective jobs, we packed up our half of the flat we had been renting in the eastern suburbs and put most of our belongings in a storage centre on the outer-outskirts of Sydney. The next week, our family and friends descended upon the two towns closest to the farm where Nick grew up in the upper Hunter Valley. We exchanged vows in an art gallery in town before bussing the crowds back to the property where we ate, drank and danced the night away in a marquee. Not even the power cutting out just before 11pm curtailed the fun of what doubled as a lavish farewell party.

That was Saturday, and by Tuesday afternoon we were at the Sydney International Airport bound for Heathrow, still riding high. We spent five nights staying with Rach, a good friend of mine from Brisbane, in Maida Vale in west London, exploring the glory of that incredible city in summer, before we headed to Croatia for our honeymoon. August was a delightful blur.

We flew back to London, where we stayed another night in Maida Vale before it was time to head to our new home. Driving into Oxford on a balmy September day felt surreal. Arriving in a foreign town for the very first time, knowing I was not merely a tourist but was set to become a resident, was an unusual feeling.

The town itself was as stunning as I'd expected. As we drove our hire-car through the cobbled streets, I caught glimpses of perfectly manicured quadrangles behind stately college entrances, dreamy spires that dotted the skyline, grand centuries-old chapels, libraries, sandstone walls covered in climbing ivy, the wide expanses of University Parks and Christchurch Meadow, and the pretty-as-a-picture canals. Everything buzzed with the energy of thousands of new residents – just like us – arriving from all corners of the country and the world to settle into their new home.

We navigated our way to the address that was to be ours for the next two years, at a University College in Summer Town, a couple of kilometres north of the city centre. To study at Oxford, each student has to be accepted into a college as well as the university itself, and our accommodation was within the 'married quarters' of the college. We had no idea what to expect, as Nick's queries had yielded few details. We assumed we would be based in a modest a semi-furnished one bedroom flat, and had kept our expectations low.

Which is why when we pulled into the street itself – stately, lined with perfectly kept, elegant Georgian homes and lush, time-chiselled trees – we figured there had been a mistake.

'Could this *really* be the right street?' I asked disbelievingly as Nick pulled our little car into the kerb.

'Well, it's definitely Staverton Road, and that's the address.'

'That plaque says University College,' I said pointing to the entranceway, 'so it must be it,' I stepped tentatively out of the car.

We stood surveying the elegant home to the left of us, and the beautiful trees lining the driveway. It was impossibly picturesque.

'Angela said to meet her in the office when we arrive,' Nick said, taking my hand as we walked down the driveway.

We followed the signs to the office, and seconds later we discovered that the grand facade was misleading. Behind the hedges and the stately home stood a collection of brutalist concrete blocks. The rectangular buildings were grey, without the slightest gesture towards design. The contrast with the facade and the rest of Oxford could not have been starker.

'I'm guessing we're going to be based here,' Nick said, pointing to one of the concrete monstrosities. 'Not there.' He laughed and pointed back to the home we had lovingly surveyed at the front.

Shortly afterwards, Angela led us through the grounds, comprised of five separate buildings spread around them, pointing out the laundry facilities, the computer rooms and various common areas. Eventually we arrived at the base of a truly ugly monolith and were led up two flights of stairs to our marital home. It was very simple and very small, not even 30 square metres, but it felt cosy. There was a bedroom, a bathroom, a small study, a kitchenette and a living area. Big windows in the study and living room meant it was well lit, and despite the fact their primary view was of another concrete monstrosity, there were trees all around us and a lush grass courtyard beneath.

Later, we came to learn that as gorgeous as the house at the front was, it comprised single-bed rooms that no student coveted because the residence was impossible to heat. Fortunately, that was a problem we never faced in our toasty little flat, even in the dead of winter.

After lugging our suitcases inside we distracted ourselves from the daunting realisation that our holiday lifestyle was coming to an end by running errand after errand. We stocked up on various household items, got phones for each of us, and Nick registered at his college. Then we spent a few days exploring our new corner of the world. We bought two second-hand bikes, the preferred mode of transport for Oxford residents, but I'd be lying if I said I enjoyed mine. I hadn't ridden a bike for more than a decade, and navigating unfamiliar roads, paths and cobblestones, often with hundreds of students whizzing by, ringing their bells for us to get out of their way, was frightening. Unlike Nick who loved every moment of each trip, I started and ended all our joint bike rides totally frazzled.

Nick's schedule was fairly full from the get-go, as it was for all new students, which made the contrast with my own schedule disarming. I had absolutely nothing to do. I didn't feel particularly well, I was vaguely nauseous and lethargic, but figured I was just adjusting to the new world order.

I made an overnight trip to London to visit a media recruiter who'd been recommended by one of my colleagues at *BRW*. Rach, my good school friend from Brisbane, whom we'd stayed with when we first arrived in London, had offered me her spare room. We had an early-morning coffee together near her flat before she headed to work and I headed to spruik my professional services. Over flat whites and toast, I confessed to her how badly I wanted to find work quickly.

'I have nothing to do,' I said. 'What did I think I was going to do once we got here?'

'You'll find a job in no time, G. I know it!'

'I hope you're right,' I said, unsure.

We spent the rest of breakfast chatting about her job in a magic circle law firm and reminiscing about our Brisbane days as uni students.

As we got up to pay, Rach smiled encouragingly. 'It's always hard at the start when you move G. Good luck, and message me after the meeting.'

Hopping off the tube and popping up into the buzz of Covent Garden at 8.45am felt wonderfully novel. Smartly dressed Londoners were all busily making their way through the cobbled streets, clutching oversized Costa or Cafe Nero takeaway cups. I wanted to know exactly where they were all headed. What were they were seeking to conquer? The atmosphere felt charged with the fresh possibilities that the early morning presents.

I had arrived early, so I meandered around the streets until the allotted time, dreaming of being able to walk into a job. I realised that I missed having an office to go to, and a job to do. I felt untethered.

Just before 9.30am, I took the elevator to the eleventh floor of a smart art deco building. The recruiter was warm, effusive and generous with his time. The purpose of the meeting was to allow me to get my head around the opportunities for journalists in the UK in general and Oxford in particular. He said that while the market was tough – the effects of the global financial crisis just a year before were still being felt keenly – my background in law and business reporting would help land me interviews, at the very least. But he offered a disclaimer: 'I would be cautiously optimistic about you being able to find work in London within a few months, but it will probably be far harder to find a role in Oxford. The jobs just aren't there in the same number. If you're willing to commute, I don't think it will take too long to find something.'

Food for thought. The afternoon before, I had caught the bus into London and it had taken just under two hours. By train, the commute was an hour and a half each way to Paddington station, but depending on the location of any office, it could be closer to two hours each way.

Unfortunately, all such practical considerations had to be put on hold because of an administrative glitch. Nick and I had got married so quickly that, as a new spouse of a new student visa holder, I couldn't have my visa approved – or start working – until November, two months away. Still, my plan was to have work lined up as soon as that box was ticked.

On the bus back to Oxford, I mulled over my options. The thought of commuting four hours a day hardly thrilled me, but what was the alternative?

I arrived home and began getting ready to meet Nick. He was at a rugby training session and partners had been invited to join the students at a pub nearby after 6pm. I was looking forward to meeting people and potentially making some friends. Except for

Rach and Nick, I had barely had contact with anyone since we arrived in Oxford.

I happily ignored my bike as I walked out the door and caught the bus into the centre of town. The bus was still something of a novelty because I loved the chance to relax and taking in the scenery of these foreign streets. Less novel was the wave of nausea that hit me just before we stopped in the centre of town. For an awful two minutes, it seemed possible that I would christen my arrival in this town by vomiting on a bus filled with neighbours I hadn't yet met.

Fortunately, I managed to avoid that indignity, but I couldn't avoid the slightly less humiliating experience of throwing up in a bin in the middle of the street.

I felt hot and sweaty and revolting. For a moment I was grateful for my anonymity, but contemplating how many *potential* friends and acquaintances might have witnessed my public display made me feel worse.

I desperately wanted to be home again, so I crossed the busy road and hopped right back on another bus headed back towards Summer Town.

Hey darling, I'm sorry I won't make it. I caught the bus into the city and ended up vomiting when I got off. I'm almost back home now.

Nick called as soon as he got my text.

'Hey, what's wrong? That sounds awful.'

I shifted a little, conscious of my fellow passengers. 'I'm really not sure. I haven't felt great for a week, but it just hit me and I had to be sick.'

'I'll hop on my bike and come home.'

'You really don't need to. Stay a bit longer. One of us has to make friends here!'

I wasn't being a martyr – I felt awful and didn't want company, and I didn't want him to miss the opportunity to make some friendships for us both.

The next morning, I still felt queasy. I tried to ignore it, but my ruse was up when I opened our small fridge and nearly fell backwards from the smell of the leftover takeaway that Nick had brought home for dinner the night before.

'Oh god!' I ran to the bathroom and threw up again.

'What is wrong with me?' I asked when I emerged a bit later. 'Do you think I have food poisoning?'

'Hmm I don't know,' he said with a curious light in his eyes. 'Do you think you might be pregnant?'

'Are you joking?' I laughed. 'As if *I* could be pregnant.'

Later that afternoon, Nick came home with a pregnancy kit, and again, I laughed when he passed the chemist bag to me.

'Imagine, if this is the moment our lives change forever!' I said, certain that it wouldn't be the case.

I sat on the toilet as I read the instructions and learned that it could take up to five minutes for a line to emerge confirming whether or not I was pregnant. The process of weeing on the stick for something so unlikely felt singularly amusing. Once it was done, I placed the plastic stick on the top of the drawers under the bathroom sink. I washed my hands, and barely thirty seconds had passed when I glanced down and saw the scariest of all sights. A LINE.

An unambiguous line.

HOLY MOTHER OF GOD.

It had to be a mistake.

I slid out of the bathroom and didn't need to say anything.

My facial expression gave it away.

'It can't be right? Can it be right? It can't be. Can you get another test?'

Nick grinned and wrapped his arms around me. 'You might be pregnant!'

He went back downstairs almost immediately and hopped back on his bike in search of another chemist. He came home with five more tests, all from different brands. I downed almost a litre of water to ensure I was hydrated enough to complete each test, one by one. They all said the same thing: I was pregnant. Back then I didn't know that there is no such thing as a false positive in a pregnancy test. I genuinely believed it was likely an error.

What are the chances that my endometriosis-addled body would fall pregnant virtually without trying? Nil. It's just not possible. The doctor said as much herself.

Except she was wrong, and so was I. A few days later, a blood test and a dating scan confirmed this wonderfully terrifying development.

The next day, Nick set off on a week-long trip to Edinburgh for Oxford's pre-season rugby tour. It had been in the diary from the very beginning and meant I was left to discover a very unique form of loneliness: I was in a new town, on the other side of the world from my family and friends, with nothing to do, and in possession of life-changing news that I couldn't fathom – and that I wasn't ready to share with anyone.

On my first morning alone, I took myself off to one of Oxford's glorious bookshops in search of some reading material. The volume of content covering pregnancy was breathtaking, and after flipping through numerous tomes, I settled on one by a midwife who had a friendly but authoritarian tone that I liked. I couldn't bring myself to even thumb the pages related to birth, but I was fascinated with the chapters outlining exactly how my tiny baby would develop.

When I went to the counter to pay, I searched the shop assistant's eyes to see whether he had any inkling of the monumental secret I was carrying. Aside from Nick and the GP, this was the only other human in the world who would have reason to know. Just holding the book felt dramatic: like it announced loudly and proudly to the whole bookshop that I was WITH CHILD.

Unsurprisingly, it appeared not to have registered with the clerk, so I walked out with my new bible wondering how I would fill the next seven days until Nick returned.

It was all very daunting, not least because of the layer of complexity it added to my employment prospects. We had been banking on me being able to earn an income to cover most of our living expenses and we had not contemplated, even for a moment, that a pregnancy might interfere with that.

And yet it happened.

Did we berate ourselves for our naivety? Of course. At length. We both felt stupid, and it was ridiculously stressful, and yet we wouldn't have changed it for the world. Having a family was something we desperately wanted.

This biological development was enough for me to decide I would seek work only in Oxford: commuting to London while I was pregnant just did not appeal. It meant accepting that I would most likely not get a job in media or journalism, which I was comfortable with. I cast the net wide and basically applied for any and every job advertised in the region in communications, policy, admin, law and research. I applied for full-time roles, contract positions and part-time jobs. If there was a job going in Oxfordshire, there was a letter with my name on it addressed to whoever was hiring.

Within weeks I had built up a hefty collection of letters thanking me for applying for these various positions and kindly letting me know that I would not be interviewed, let alone needed. It threw me. Aside from not having contemplated pregnancy, I had also not contemplated being unemployed.

I knew rejection letters from recruiters and prospective employers were not a helpful yardstick to measure my identity by, and I knew I shouldn't take it personally. I knew, on paper, that I was more than the job I did or didn't have, but, my god, I had a lot of free time to wonder, and in weaker moments it was hard not to conclude the worst.

Being pregnant compounded the fear and rejection: as every week passed, I got closer to having an actual baby. If I couldn't get a job before then, how the hell was I ever going to get one afterwards?

The power of honesty

October 2009

Outside it was overcast and looked as chilly as it had started to feel. Our dining room table was adjacent to a window that took up the length of the wall, giving us an uninterrupted view of the courtyard. The trees were dropping their leaves, creating a thick golden carpet speckled with dots of fiery red on top of the lawn. From the second floor, I had a bird's-eye view of the comings and goings on the small campus: students weaving across the grass towards the bike shed, exiting the computer room with printed notes under their arms, carrying baskets of washing in and out of the laundry. They carried on busily while I sat at the table with my laptop, a cup of milky tea and some toast. My to-do list comprised a single task: find a job. It had been the same for weeks, and I was working towards submitting another set of job applications when I stumbled upon a document with the file name 'Letter.doc'. I opened it expecting to find a cover letter, hopeful it might be good enough to at least land me an interview somewhere.

Instead I found a desperate cry for help that had never been sent.

The week before that very first vertigo attack struck in my office, the law firm had hosted a client event for women in business that I'd attended. The guest speaker was Mia Freedman, a former magazine editor and newspaper columnist who I had admired from afar, and who spoke honestly and humorously about her career. She had just resigned from Channel 9 in a blaze of unfavourable publicity and was unsure of her next move. She seemed vulnerable and self-assured at once.

I was captivated by her presence and her story, and after listening to her speak I went straight back to my desk and started writing her a letter, which was both sad and shocking to read two and half years later. I knew even then that I wanted out of law, and to my desperate eyes, Mia represented a life raft.

I never finished the letter. The following week was the beginning of the end for my career in law, and as my life careered off that cliff, I completely forgot about the letter.

That is, until that October day in Oxford in 2009. Reading it was revelatory. It was tangible proof of how deeply lost I had been at that point.

> *Dear Mia,*
> *You recently attended a young business forum hosted by my employer, and I was inspired. Your honesty, insight and success were overwhelming.*
>
> *I was surprised to hear that the catalyst for your break into the world of magazines was a humble letter to Lisa Wilkinson … and now here I am, trying that same technique. They do say imitation is the greatest form of flattery.*

I am eighteen months through a graduate law program. I completed a bachelor of law and business (public relations) at the Queensland University of Technology in 2005 and was admitted to practice as a solicitor in New South Wales in 2006. But here I am in 2007, in seemingly typical Gen-Y fashion, wanting to pull the plug on law.

Law was tempting: it was structured, offered great potential and looked impressive on my CV. But the honeymoon is well and truly over and I can no longer ignore my doubts. (I can't go out anymore without looking at other people's careers with predatory desire.)

The former NSW premier Bob Carr, another former journalist, also recently attended a function at my firm and spoke about acting on passion when making career decisions. You made a similar remark about people being honest with themselves about what is in their blood. It was that comment that sparked me to think.

I am confident that if given an opportunity I could build a satisfying career as a journalist.

It ended there, and while I didn't ever make my way to 'the ask', it's clear where I was headed: *Please take me under your wing.*

After taking my words in, I felt compelled – and emboldened – to start a new letter to Mia, who by this point was publishing her increasingly popular blog *Mamamia* I wasn't ready to put my name on it, but I was ready to be honest about what had happened to me, so I forgot about job applications and instead wrote a CliffsNotes version of my nervous breakdown.

I started by explaining to Mia that I had just discovered

the unsent letter, originally sparked by seeing her speak. I said I remembered thinking that if I sent her a letter, in the same vein as the one she penned to Lisa Wilkinson to get her break, then maybe she would rescue me from the career that was making me miserable.

I explained that I never finished or sent the letter because my regular life was soon interrupted and didn't resume anything akin to normal transmission for many, many months. I explained the vertigo, my Crohn's disease, the countless doctors, the myriad tests, the diets and the fruitless search for answers. I explained that I landed in a psychiatric hospital, got diagnosed with anxiety and gradually started to feel better both physically and mentally.

Before I had a chance to second-guess myself, I put the sixteen-hundred-word missive into an email and pressed send. I had found an email address for Mia on the website, but I honestly wasn't even sure she would receive it. That night, as we went to bed, I sent it to Nick. At this point having the internet on our phones was still a novelty, so we read it together.

'Darling it's amazing. I hope she reads it and publishes it.'
'Me too.'
'You will be a famous author before you know it.'
'Unlikely!' I laughed.

As ever, Nick had more faith in my potential than I did, and while I didn't believe him, I did like having his backing. He was aware of what I'd left behind in Sydney: neither of us had envisioned me being unemployed, which is partly why the idea of something giving me a boost was so welcome.

The next morning when I woke to a reply from her I was gobsmacked. Not only had she received it, but she also wanted to share it with her readers – if that was okay with me.

'Mia read it! And she's going to publish it as an anonymous

guest post! *Eeeeek.*

Nick smiled sleepily. 'That's awesome! Well done!' He rolled over and wrapped his arms around me. 'By the way, I told you so!' he said, and we both laughed.

The next week it went live, and even though it was anonymous, it still felt like I had taken a gigantic leap of faith. Seeing my words published for the world was terrifying. While I had been relatively open with close friends about what I had experienced in the past few years, this was far more revealing. I had laid myself entirely bare.

Within a few hours the piece had a hundred comments, which I read and re-read a thousand times over the coming days. That my story had resonated with strangers buoyed me enough to share it with Mum, Belinda and a couple of my closest friends. In some ways, sharing it with them was scarier than sharing it with the anonymous masses. I was telling the people I loved the honest, ugly truth about what had happened.

My leap of faith felt rewarded, because the response from friends and strangers alike was unanimous: being candid about my struggles was not gratuitous, it was helpful.

In time, I grew brave enough to not just tell my story, but to put my name to it in print and in person. Every time I did, the response was the same. Other people before and after me have had similar experiences. Breakdowns might not be universal, but they are more prolific than you might guess. Sometimes life continues on and many of those around the sufferer are none the wiser. Sometimes, like in my case, life effectively stops.

When I was falling apart, I was convinced I was the only person to have succumbed the way I did; I was humiliated that it had gone so far. I was ashamed that with all the privileges

I had, I still couldn't cope. Being honest about my experience stripped back the shame I had felt so keenly back then. There was a time I believed 'shame' was reserved exclusively for people who had committed truly shameful acts – murder, rape, abusing children. I was wrong. Shame is something we all carry and it can be debilitating.

Years later, I was startled to read a theory by Dr Brené Brown that the antidote to shame is vulnerability. My experience perfectly aligned with that idea.

When I fell apart, I was forced into being vulnerable: being in rehab made me think about myself very differently, and I had to accept that what had happened had happened. At the end I decided – quite consciously – to be okay with having not been okay. There was no other pathway I could envisage. Accepting my failings and flaws ran counter to all of my pre-breakdown instincts, but being vulnerable is what facilitated my shift from shame into acceptance.

Speaking about my breakdown made me less embarrassed about what had happened. Telling my story made me recognise that rather than being a source of indignity, it was a source of hope. Even pride.

Sharing my story anonymously on an Australian website made it clear that there was real power in being vulnerable. It didn't render the experience of being unemployed and desperately seeking work easy, but it did give me something of a psychological safety net. It reminded me of where I had been and planted the tiny seed I needed to remember that even without a job I had value.

My first bite at employment came in late November, three months after I began looking, after I realised that temp work was the only realistic option. Within an hour of emailing one agency,

I got a phone call asking if I could pop in. I was nearby at the time but since it was snowing I was dressed in wellington boots and jeans – hardly suitable job interview attire. A bubbly recruiter called Dawn told me to come in anyway because they needed someone to take on a week as a receptionist at a nearby helicopter base, and the job started on Monday.

When I arrived, Dawn told me – deadpan – that all they needed was someone to look very nice at the desk. I swallowed my pride and said that if they were willing to overlook my swollen stomach, that should be okay. She asked if I would come by on Monday morning before work so they could check I looked 'nice enough'. I resisted the temptation to ask whether she had seen from my CV that I had spent a quite few years in professional offices and was capable of dressing myself appropriately (even if I wasn't capable of securing a job).

I went along with it and popped in on the Monday morning, where my appearance was approved. After heading off to the base, I had my duties explained to me, begrudgingly, by the permanent receptionist, who was eager to head off on leave for a week.

'Thanks to new management the company's extremely tight. They don't even buy decent biscuits anymore, the Christmas party was cancelled this year and they barely give you a lunch break,' she said, getting me up to speed. 'Oh, and the new management are German.'

She could well have said vermin.

She told me which office romances to watch and who was in the process of being made redundant before finally 'warning' me about a transgender employee. 'She's worked here for fifteen years, the first twelve of those she was a he and now she is a she. But the doctor hasn't done a great job. If it were me I'd ask for my money back. Wait till you see her. She still looks like a man but we can't really say that.'

No, you really can't.

From there she proceeded to explain my tasks: answer phones, transfer calls and sort the mail. In detailing the mailing procedure, she surreptitiously pointed out a stash of boxes under the desk of all shapes and sizes.

'I sell quite a few things on eBay,' she said by way of explanation. 'Keep all of those boxes hidden right under the desk until the postman arrives and hand them over at the very last minute.'

I got the impression her side-business might not have been company-approved.

Her phone demonstration was enlightening. She barked into the handset each time it rang, leaving the caller under no illusion that their phonecall was a rude and unwelcome intrusion into her day. Had I not witnessed these exchanges, I would not have believed the number of callers who, upon hearing my Australian accent at the other end of the line, were immediately taken aback. Was I new? Was the witch gone? Where's the angry lady? I heard these questions from staff and clients alike on an hourly basis.

My stint was so successful that I was invited back to the helicopter base on a semi-regular basis. It turned out to be the best job I had while in England, which is saying something. Aside from mourning my *BRW* job I just desperately wanted something to do: being productive and having something – *anything* – to do was far more enjoyable than being idle.

Mindless temp work was not without its challenges though, particularly because we were living in a university town filled with uber-bright residents who were conquering their professional dreams one degree at a time, often while simultaneously running charitable foundations, taking part in triathlons and being frighteningly personable, social and well-adjusted individuals.

'What are you studying?' was the well-intentioned question I grew to resent slightly less than I resented the inevitable follow-up when I said that it was my husband who was studying: 'Oh great, so where are you working?'

A five-day assignment at a luxury car dealership was particularly painful. The agency and I were both under the impression I was being hired to man the reception desk, which we later learned was not exactly the case. Upon arriving, I was welcomed by a young English girl and told that I could sit beside her at reception.

In front of her was a computer, a telephone, some pens, paper, some post-it notes – all of the typical office trimmings. In front of *me* was a wide expanse of empty desk. No phone, no computer, not even a pen. I awaited my instructions. A few minutes passed before the girl explained that the service manager – who ran the service workshop across the street – was on holiday for a week.

That's nice that he's getting a break from work, I thought. *But what's that got to do with me?*

She went on to explain that in his absence, her workload would increase substantially – she would be responsible for booking in all the car services and managing the timings for each job, she'd thought it would be good to have some assistance at reception. It sounded reasonable enough, until I actually began the work.

The receptionist's phone would ring, then I would quickly pick it up and answer 'Good morning, [insert luxury car dealership name] Oxford, Georgie speaking.' The caller would then articulate his or her needs, at which point, regardless of what those needs were, I would have to say, 'One moment, please, I'll just transfer you to our … receptionist.' At that point I would 'transfer' (as in, literally pass her the phone) and she would process their call. Without a computer or phone of my own, I was unable to do anything except feel comically superfluous. I began to wonder if I was part of a sketch entitled 'A Guide to the UK's failing economy'.

My only other job was to record the time of each call and nature of their query. This would be quite fine assuming the phone rang off the hook. But it didn't. By 10.15am the phone had rung once. Around this time, my colleague noticed that my presence might in fact be unnecessary.

'Is this a little bit boring for you?' she asked.

'Well, I could certainly do more if there is anything else that needs doing?'

'No. That's fine,' she said.

So I sat there, willing the time to pass. It got worse when a smarmy manager came in with a group of associates, took one look at my pregnant belly and asked exactly what I'd done to get myself in that state. They all laughed; I wanted to disappear.

Later, another salesman came over.

'Love, do you reckon you're up to making me and my co-worker a cup of tea,' he asked really slowly, as if he had just posed the biggest professional challenge a person could ever face.

I was tempted to ask him to show me how to make the first cup and then I could probably manage to make the second, but instead I jumped up, ran to the kitchen and made two cups of tea really, really slowly. I was grateful for having something to do.

It was a long week that ended in tears.

'They treat me like I am a total moron and I have *nothing* to do so they probably all think I am a total moron,' I wailed to Nick on the Friday night, before we left to attend a college dinner with a group of Australian girls I'd befriended – smart, funny, kind girls, all of whom were studying at Oxford. 'Everyone else here is so clever, doing amazing things, and I've got to sit there having men ask me if I know how to make a cup of tea. A cup of tea?!'

'Georgie you are as smart and capable as every other person here and everyone who has met you knows that,' he said.

'Not the people at the car dealership. And no one I have sent my CV to since we've been here has thought that.'

'I hate that you have had to put up with this rubbish all week and I hate that finding work has been so hard, but it's not a reflection of who you are. It's a reflection of our circumstances here. You are the same person as when we left Sydney: you have the same brain and the same personality and everything that made you successful at *BRW* is the same.'

I didn't entirely believe him, but I knew he had a point. I also knew that me not being able to find work was playing heavily on Nick: I had travelled across the world to support his dream, but we hadn't really envisioned that it might not be easy for me.

Eventually, as the weeks and months clocked over, I came to realise that I had to think of this as a temporary arrangement. We wouldn't live here forever; this was just another chapter in life, and taking everything a day at a time was all I could do.

It did help to remember that I had endured worse. The fact I had managed to muster some self-esteem while I was in rehab made me believe I could find some of that while living overseas with a husband I adored and a healthy baby in utero. There was a time when that had seemed entirely out of reach.

Achieving that clarity wasn't the easiest of hurdles to clear – there was plenty of fear and inadequacy to wade through – but eventually I did.

It might have been a little earlier than most, but what I experienced in those first few months of our life overseas is something that I subsequently discovered many, many women go through on first becoming mothers. In the 21st century, the vast majority of women who fall pregnant are working, so maternity leave is often the first extended break they have ever had from the workforce. To say it's an emotional and physical minefield is an understatement.

There are two transitions that effectively occur simultaneously in this setting: a woman loses a large part of her identity that has underpinned her sense of self and purpose, and it's at the exact moment that she takes on a new role that is entirely unfamiliar, relentless and all-consuming – and for which she is not yet qualified. On having a baby, a woman often becomes more isolated than she's ever been at exactly the moment she needs support more than ever. Both changes require wholesale adjustment, and dismissing either as trivial is cruel.

In time I would come to conclude that I was lucky to navigate these hurdles separately, in that I was effectively unemployed for my whole pregnancy, getting that adjustment and identity crisis out of the way before I dove into actual motherhood. But back when I was wandering the cobbled streets of Oxford, getting bigger by the day, desperately looking for work, I had no way of knowing that.

I felt like a great chunk of my identity had gone AWOL, and if I said it wasn't disconcerting, I'd be lying. From Oxford, my brief foray into journalism seemed like a distant dream. A fluke.

An inestimable blessing

May 2010

'Nick! Something's definitely happening.'

It was 6.30am on the 25th of May 2010, and I'd been lying awake since 5am experiencing fairly regular contortions in my abdomen. I felt funny. It was my due date, so being in labour was the obvious explanation, but I knew from our antenatal classes that giving birth rarely happens as quickly as movies and TV shows have led us all to believe.

After an hour and a half monitoring these cramp-like sensations, I deemed it time to wake Nick up.

He woke up with a start. 'What is it?'

'I don't really know.'

'Should we go to hospital?' he said, sitting up with a wide grin spreading across his face.

'I don't think so. Not yet. But I've been having weird contraction things every ten minutes since 5am.'

All of this felt deeply surreal. I had been pregnant for exactly forty weeks by this point, but I still could not fathom that my body – the very same body that I had viewed as entirely defunct for almost a decade – could conceive and grow a baby, and by accident!

Despite my fear, I was in awe of it too: physically my pregnancy really was a dream, and it all felt a bit like the universe was rewarding me for my body's myriad dysfunctions.

Of course the reward for a perfectly straightforward, enjoyable pregnancy was the labour from hell.

Like many women before me, and likely many after, I was simply not prepared for what our first child's foray into the world would entail. For a long time afterwards, my reaction to those stories about mums who deliver babies in the car on the way to hospital because their labour is so short involved intense pangs of insane, visceral jealousy. I was glad to hear they were okay, of course, but why were they so anatomically well-equipped to deliver a baby so fast? What kind of sweet deal did they strike with mother nature? WHERE WAS I WHEN THEY WERE DIVVYING OUT THOSE ARRANGEMENTS?

My contractions started at ten-minute intervals at 5am, and by 9am they were five minutes apart. They were strong from the get-go and they never got further apart. Every childbirth book and antenatal teacher will tell you that the point at which contractions are just five minutes apart is the time to get to hospital. It's not uncommon for contractions to begin at thirty minutes apart then whittle down to five minutes and then, as the final stage approaches, just a minute or less apart. So when mine started that close together I could only conclude one thing: my baby was coming fast.

It wasn't. My baby was coming but, my god, it was going to take its time. Theoretically I could have driven from Sydney to Perth and still have made it to a hospital in plenty of time to deliver our firstborn. I assumed I'd be raring to go by the twelve-hour mark, and yet I had not even dilated. Not one bit. Not a single centimetre. It seemed my cervix totally missed the memo. After twenty-four hours with barely any progress beyond being dilated a paltry two centimetres, I was exhausted and disheartened. By twenty-eight hours I was barely lucid, and after suggesting someone put me down like an animal, an anaesthetist promptly arrived to put me out of my misery. Fortunately, he dismissed my suggestion and opted for the less drastic intervention: an epidural.

Once the epidural had been administered, I was intensely grateful for the anaesthetist's very existence, and for the marvels of modern medicine. The wretched pain was gone. I was finally able to relax while the wonders of medicine hurried my cervix along, and it was heaven. I dozed on and off, excited and shattered.

Then, after five hours, the epidural wore off down one side of my body – like, in a straight line completely down the middle. So while my right side was free to bask in pain-free contractions, the left side experienced the increasingly frequent and violent spasms in all of their painful glory.

After an hour trying to figure this quirk out, they decided to just top the epidural right up, which worked a treat at disarming the pain but was diabolical in every other way. I was so nauseous that I vomited on the darling midwife who had been by my side for the past fifteen hours, and I felt so drugged that I barely knew where I was.

I was hot, cold and shaky. I wanted to cry and laugh and cuddle everyone. I confessed my undying love to every midwife who looked my way. I begged Nick to never leave me. Like not even ever leave the room.

But even in my drug-addled fog, I realised when the atmosphere changed. It happened very quickly: one minute everyone was happy and relaxed, and the next minute no one was talking. People kept emerging, machines were wheeled in and the big boss was called.

'Your baby is showing some signs of distress,' the obstetrician told me, staring into my eyes. 'You will either push this baby out in the next ten minutes or I will be doing an emergency C-section. Do you understand?'

I did, and I was as desperate to do what she asked as I was totally unable to do it. I was flummoxed. The epidural had cut any connection between my brain and body, and when she said 'push' I could barely understand her.

Pushing a feather was beyond my function at that point, and the result was a forceps delivery, after which I was proud, torn, shattered and delirious. And by delirious I mean truly delirious – not delirious with love or joy – I actually felt like I was inhabiting a distant and unfamiliar planet.

The prize for this hell was a baby girl whom we immediately named Isabella Grace, and she was absolutely perfect. A content, tiny little bundle who was ours. But I remained in a state of shock.

'Why would anyone ever do that more than once?' I asked my mum in a conversation the day after I'd had Issy.

'I know, darling. It's a miracle,' she said.

It really is.

Two of my best friends in Oxford visited us in hospital the next day and, eight years on, they are still visibly shaken when they recall what they saw. So long without sleep and a marathon labour meant I was a terrifying sight to behold. Contraceptive in effect.

My physically compromised state was naturally compounded by the fact I was now responsible for feeding a living, breathing baby around the clock with my very broken body. (Our seasoned antenatal teacher shared one piece of wisdom in this regard that I will never forget: childbirth would be much easier if you didn't become responsible for a newborn baby immediately afterwards, and, equally, caring for a newborn baby would be much easier if you weren't recovering from the physical demands of delivering that newborn.)

The good news was that after a hellishly long and brutal birth, we took receipt of a baby very fond of feeding *and* sleeping. Not every single night, and there were plenty of wobbles, but, on the whole, she was a decidedly content little girl, which made our rather hasty descent into parenthood a tiny bit less shocking.

Both of our parents visited and helped out and, fortuitously, she was born in the long summer break, which meant Nick had less on than ever before.

Issy's arrival – obviously – markedly changed my daily existence. I was able to let go of my angst about filling my days because this project filled them all. (And more.) I no longer had as much free time to troubleshoot my employability, and I had a very clear purpose: keeping this tiny human alive.

Despite the obvious inconvenience of having a baby while Nick was a university student, the upside was that he was around. His study commitments were significant, but particularly in the first few months of her life, he had near-total autonomy about how and when he got his work done, which meant we were free to fumble our way through parenting life together. Caring for Issy really was a joint endeavour, so while I was responsible for the breastfeeding, I barely changed a nappy for the first few months of her life.

But there were challenges too.

A low point transpired when Nick had to travel to Russia for an eleven-day rugby tour, which just happened to coincide with the only ten days in Issy's life when she refused to feed or sleep. We had no family in the country, and while I hadn't expected my solo parenting stint with our three-month-old to be a breeze, I was floored by what it involved.

The days were interminably long twenty-four-hour cycles, in which I grappled with my still-unfamiliar and suddenly miserable infant. The processes of feeding her and putting her to bed were ordinarily quite lovely, but no more. When I tried to feed her she grabbed at my hair, scratched at my chest, yanked painfully on and off my nipple and writhed around. She wouldn't stay attached for longer than a few minutes. If she fell asleep at all during the day she usually woke screaming not long afterwards. Mostly she would only sleep on me, and even then not for long.

Even when she did sleep, rest eluded me. I lay in bed fretting, anticipating her next waking and what I'd face. I was basically counting the hours until Nick returned. I fantasised about him coming home early. I pictured my mum miraculously turning up in the country, in our flat, ready to help.

For almost a full week, I persisted: Issy and I were as sleep-deprived, distraught and crotchety as each other. Whatever confidence I had developed as a new mum was entirely eroded. I had no idea what I was doing and no idea where I could get help.

The local community centre in our suburb ran a free baby yoga class on a Monday morning that I had attended a few times. 'Baby yoga' is a very generous description of the activity. Mostly it consisted of some super-gentle yoga moves for the mums, singing a few songs to babies, and then sitting in a circle sharing a cup of tea and biscuits. On this occasion, the teacher asked us to go around in a circle and describe our last week. I considered playing my week down, but when it was my turn I couldn't help but blurt out my woes. Tears flooded down my face as I explained that I could no longer make my baby happy. I couldn't feed her properly. I couldn't settle her properly. I couldn't get her to sleep. I didn't know how to be a mum anymore and I felt so alone. I said my husband was in another country and my family were all on the other side of the world.

What followed was something I have seen replicated many times since, but it still, eight and a bit years later, moves me to tears. The women in that class rallied behind me in every way I needed. One immediately took Issy from my arms and began rocking her. The teacher rang the hospital and organised an appointment for me in the free lactation clinic that afternoon. Another mum offered to come with me and Issy to the appointment. There were hugs and shared tears and so many kind and encouraging words. Later that day there were meals dropped off and chocolates delivered to my door. There were text messages and follow-ups. I was overwhelmed with help, support and solidarity.

The lactation specialist certainly wasn't warm, but the orders she barked at me about the way I was holding my baby and allowing her to latch made a difference. I had been cradling Issy like she was a newborn and needed to give her three-month-old body more space. This tweak meant that, gradually, she returned to having longer feeds again, and began sleeping again for longer than twenty minutes at a time.

As fate would have it, the night Nick arrived home at 9pm, ready to clock on for what I had promised him would be a busy night feeding and resettling, Issy slept till 7am.

I kid you not.

~

With the exception of Issy's birth, the most unforgettable day of our time living in the UK took place on the 10th of December in 2010 when the annual varsity match between Oxford and Cambridge was held at Twickenham stadium in London. It's a historic fixture that's been played for more than 130 years, which meant 30,000 spectators turned out to watch what was to be the final rugby match of Nick's sporting career. In January he'd been elected captain, so had led the team all the way through the season that builds up to this one game.

If anyone had ever told me that a game of football – any game – would rate as one of the most emotional, exhilarating and memorable experiences of my life, I'd have assumed they'd mistaken me for someone else. But sitting in those stands, with the community of friends we'd made, with family who'd travelled to watch and our contented, rugged-up baby girl in my arms, watching Nick lead his team to a nail-biting victory? That was definitely me.

While I played no part in the triumph on the field, I knew the victory was mine too, and I felt proud. Nick and I had arrived in Oxford a year and a half earlier knowing no one. Since then we had faced a surprise pregnancy, an unexpected stint of unemployment that had made us financially reliant on family in ways neither of us had expected or wanted, and we'd become parents. Now, Nick was just one term away from securing his

Masters, we had both made great friends and we'd built a life we loved. Reflecting on all of that was enough to make me cry a flood of happy tears when I made my way down through the crowds to Nick after the game finished.

He was still on the field, muddy and sweaty and beaming with pride. His eyes lit up when he caught sight of Issy in my arms and me walking towards him.

'You did it!" I said with a smile a mile wide, leaning over the railing to the field. 'I can't believe you did it!'

He jumped over the railing, took Issy off me and wrapped his arms around us both.

'You made this happen, darling,' he whispered in my ear. 'Thank you for everything you've done here. I can't wait to celebrate!'

His grin was even bigger than mine. Issy was delightfully oblivious to the specifics but revelling in the madness around her, flapping her little arms happily.

Two thoughts lingered as I made my way back up the stairs with Issy to our group to get the celebrations underway. First, we made a good team. Second, thank god he ignored me all those years ago.

~

When Issy was seven months old, I finally took a leap and started a blog. The very first week we had arrived in Oxford, unbeknown to anyone, I had actually set up the backend of a blog. I had toyed with the idea of having a creative outlet, but I was embarrassed to admit that to anyone, let alone publish something, and two questions ultimately kept my blog dormant.

Who exactly do you think you are? Why would anyone want to read anything you have to say?

By the time Issy was seven months old, I finally lost interest in fighting these questions.

Who exactly did I think I was? A person who wanted to write a blog.

Why would anyone want to read anything I had to say? They might not.

My morale was boosted because we were on the home stretch of a unique chapter. I found some mettle in the little things I had achieved: meaningful friendships, overcoming the self-doubt and uncertainty that the first few months here involved, supporting Nick, having a baby on the other side of the world.

It seems strange to have found confidence in my role as a new mum when baby-rearing was so laden with insecurity and doubt, but, strangely, it did buffer my self-worth. Despite the fact it was overwhelming and I often felt out of my depth, being a mother added something to what I saw and valued in myself. I was patient and generous and fun with Issy. And parenthood gave me *plenty* to write about. I felt like I had stepped into a foreign land, one that I hadn't previously known existed.

When Issy was a newborn, writing a blog wasn't something I actively considered, immersed as I was in the 24/7 role of caring for her. But once she was sleeping regularly for long stretches of the day, I suddenly felt like I had time on my hands that I didn't want to spend folding laundry. *Anything* but laundry.

One Sunday night, over dinner at our flat, Nick brought this subject up with a small group of my girlfriends, all of whom encouraged me to get writing, and *Not Another Blogging Mother* was born the very next day. I posted three or four times a week about everything from motherhood, to feminism, to the royal family, to life in Oxford, and I derived more joy from my tiny corner of the worldwide web than I had ever imagined. Having been in the wilderness creatively, it was intoxicating to connect with my brain again. My audience was modest, but it grew steadily and the engagement it brought me with friends, family and strangers from near and far was quite genuinely life-affirming. It filled up my bucket and gave me confidence and contentment I had never expected.

The lesson was compelling. I had survived the mental idleness that unemployment provoked, but there is a chasm between merely surviving and thriving. Having a pursuit that engaged my mind made the difference: it felt like my world opened up again, and I was happier and lighter because of it. I enjoyed being a mum even more for the contrast the writing added to my days with Issy. On top of that, Nick and I each having our own pursuits felt like a better natural fit for us.

The difference in my demeanour and headspace was obvious, and if either Nick or I needed any further proof that I am better off with purpose, we had it.

Unexpectedly, my blog also proved quite handy for the changes coming in my professional life.

In June of 2011, a month before we were set to return to Sydney, one of my colleagues from *BRW* got in touch over Facebook.

'Hey, Georgie, I know you guys are moving back soon. Just flagging that I'm going on mat leave in August and *BRW* is looking for a replacement. You should apply!'

I felt oddly nervous as I contemplated the possibility of returning to *BRW*. I can't really explain why I hadn't considered this a likelihood

– I had departed on positive terms after all – but I had been so untethered from the workforce that it seemed far-fetched.

As luck would have it, I was spending a few days in Rome with my mum and Issy, giving Nick space to prepare for his final assessments, when I heard the good news. Kate Mills, the new editor who had been the deputy when I left, offered me a maternity-leave contract to work four days a week, starting three weeks after we were set to return. A dream come true.

The next hurdle – finding suitable childcare for Issy – was less dreamy. I began emailing childcare centres all around Sydney, and was knocked back by each of them. It was like applying for jobs all over again, but this time it was my sweet little toddler getting rejected – and they hadn't even met her!

My naivety was precious, but until that time I had honestly believed that childcare would be like primary school, with a spot for every child. How else were parents supposed to work?

Eventually I woke to an email with a positive reply, and Issy was offered four days of care a week at a Montessori centre: the only catches were that the centre was based in the heart of the CBD and cost $156 dollars a day. Neither Nick nor I would be working from the CBD, so we'd literally be travelling to the centre of the city by bus to drop our toddler off in a high-rise building, then come back to collect her after work. The cost was eye-watering: we were to be spending more on childcare than rent, which is no mean feat in Sydney. Our monthly childcare bill also represented something of a blow to our capacity to save, but there was no alternative. Aside from the financial necessity, Nick and I knew firsthand the price of me not working, and it wasn't worth it. Our lives would be better served with both of us engaged.

At this time, Nick and I were genuinely surprised, on a regular basis, at the assumptions people made about us both as parents. He would be greeted with a virtual ticker-tape parade for taking Issy to the park on a Sunday morning, whereas I would be greeted with evil eyes and cutting commentary should Issy so much as squawk on our bus ride to childcare.

These expectations were comically apparent when Nick took Issy for a little week-long excursion out of the city. Her childcare centre closed the week before Christmas, and because I was having two weeks off *after* Christmas, we needed to fill the care gap for one week. Nick had been posted to Wagga Wagga, five hours from Sydney, for a three-month rotation as part of his intern year and discovered there was a centre opposite the Base Hospital that could take her for the week. On the Sunday evening they drove down, and from the moment they arrived, Nick was bombarded with questions and offers of help.

'Where is her mother?'

'How long are you in charge of her?'

'Can we help?'

Needless to say, in the almost three months I had been carrying the parenting load solo in Sydney, no one asked me where her father was or how long I would be in charge. Lovely friends and relatives *were* forthcoming with lovely offers of help, which I accepted, but these weren't extended from the position of it being unfathomable that I could work and keep a tiny human alive. In Nick's case, colleagues of various ages, jobs and genders were astonished that he might be capable of pulling it off.

On the upside, the experience of returning to *BRW* was almost better than when I had first begun as a researcher, heightened as it was by my newfound appreciation of being able to attend the bathroom alone, drinking coffee while it was hot and engaging in stimulating conversation with adults. Everything I had loved about the job the first time around – the interviews, the writing, the editorial process and the team – remained as satisfying as ever. At the end of the maternity-leave contract, I was offered a permanent position.

My contentment meant I didn't ever question the rigmarole of taking Issy on the bus twice a day in peak hour or forking out vast sums of money each week, but I did question – frequently – the structural challenge that inadequate childcare poses to working parents. I questioned often how this and other issues prevented women, and it was mostly women, from progressing in workplaces. I was fascinated by the double standards women and men faced as parents. Fixated isn't too strong a word to describe my interest in the subject of women and gender equality. My eyes were opened, and once I had seen the inequality I couldn't unsee it.

I was pitching stories constantly about the gender gap: the pay gap, sexism, the dismal number of women in senior leadership roles, inadequate childcare. Kate Mills supported my interest and accepted many of my pitches for features, though occasionally she had cause to remind me to consider other ideas too. Within a job I already loved, I had found a niche I was passionate about.

It's time to be you

March 2013

Georgie,
We haven't met in person but I'd like to meet you for a coffee to talk about a job. Can you please send me your number so we can try and line up a time?
Marina.

It was 8pm on a Saturday night and I was sitting on our sofa breastfeeding our second daughter, Lulu, who was four months old, when my phone lit up with a Twitter notification. I had received a private message from Marina Go, the launch publisher of a newish website called *Women's Agenda*, published by Private Media, which I had read from the day it went live eight months earlier. It was an intelligent combination of news and commentary aimed at women, and was fast gaining respect and admirers like myself. While Marina and I hadn't met, we had followed one another on Twitter for several months. Admittedly, there wasn't much competition, but her message made my Saturday night: my heart stopped when I read it.

At this point, Nick had inched closer to his professional dream of becoming a reconstructive surgeon. At the end of his resident year, a few months earlier, he'd successfully applied for a position as a plastics registrar. The job was at a busy hospital that was a forty-five-minute drive from our flat in no traffic, and up to an hour and a half in peak hour. His roster was particularly brutal and involved working three weekends out of every four, in addition to working Monday to Friday from 7am till well past 7pm.

This was one of the rare one-in-four weekends that Nick had off work, but one of his school friends was getting married a few hours outside Sydney, and children were strictly not allowed. The venue was thirty minutes from the nearest town and we just couldn't swing the logistics for me to go. If I said I cheerfully embraced the opportunity to have yet more time parenting on my own I'd be lying, which is also why Marina's message was so welcome. Perhaps there was life beyond this baby?

Welcoming a baby the second time around, our family arrangement was very different to our little university student nirvana in Oxford. For starters, little Lulu surprised us by arriving seamlessly nearly three weeks early. It wasn't a speedy labour, but I didn't miss a night's sleep and the epidural worked well enough to numb the pain but not so well that I couldn't push. I didn't need forceps, and her birth was a legitimately amazing experience. That night as I held her in my arms, I couldn't quite believe that all I could think about was how much I wanted to relive it. To do it all again. *Finally* I understood why some women say childbirth is empowering, and why the planet remains populated.

My parents flew to Sydney that day to meet their newest grandchild and to mind Issy, who was smitten from the moment she clapped eyes on the dark-haired, puffy newborn on my chest. That evening I was higher than I'd ever felt with love, relief and gratitude.

After several long feeds, Lulu spent some of that first evening in the hospital's night nursery. Early the next morning, a midwife delivered her back to me.

'That's the loudest baby we have ever had in this nursery,' she said, looking me square in the eyes. Given the midwife appeared to be in her fifties, and we were in a major maternity hospital, I couldn't seek solace in the possibility she was drawing from a limited sample size. I'm not superstitious, but her words struck me as singularly ominous: a sign of bad things to come. They were.

Blessed as I was with a dreamy birth and a second healthy baby, it was probably only fair that I took receipt of a tiny human who was not only exceptionally loud but exceptionally eager to test out that volume. Two facts that have remained unchanged.

Volume aside, the primary challenge for me adjusting to life with a newborn again was that I also had a toddler to care for, and my co-parent was largely unavailable. During the day my hands were full, and navigating the famed witching hours from 4pm to 7pm (if I was lucky) with a single set of hands to meet the very physical demands of feeding, bathing and putting a toddler and a baby to bed was a feat. Neither of our families lived in Sydney and we were living on a single income, so help wasn't an option. While I could manage the days and the early evenings as a solo operator fairly well (with chocolate and coffee my daily vices), the nights always tested me.

Even from the very beginning, Issy had always slept for at least one decent stretch a night, which guaranteed me a chunk of rest if I hopped into bed early. When she did wake throughout the night, Nick would bring her to me for a feed and then change her nappy, re-swaddle her and return her to bed, at which point she would promptly fall back asleep. (This routine stemmed from the quite handy fact I am an incredibly deep sleeper, so Nick would often hear Issy wake before I did.)

Second time around, I had a baby who would never sleep for more than three hours in a row, took a lot longer to resettle after a feed, refused both dummy and bottle, *and* my night-time buddy wasn't around to step in. In the first half of Lulu's first year of life, it wasn't uncommon for Nick to arrive home after midnight. Given the hours he was working and his daily commute, I was anxious for him to get as much sleep as possible, so I would make him wear earplugs. On the nights he was home early he stepped in without question, but those occasions were few and far between. The sleep deprivation was tough.

To complicate matters, I was also experiencing excruciating pain in my right hip on a regular basis. When Lulu was twelve weeks old, I had slipped down a flight of stairs and landed hard, right on my bottom, when I was leaving a friend's place. Fortunately, my friend had been cradling Lulu at the time, and Issy, whose hand I'd held as I tripped down the staircase, remained unscathed. The girls weren't hurt, but I was. Issy burst into tears with worry, and I quickly set about reassuring her that I was fine. I strapped both the girls in their car seats before heading home, confident my discomfort would ease with time. It didn't. When the ache continued beyond a few days, I visited a physiotherapist for treatment. But it would be a long time before I found relief.

A low point transpired with a surprise visitor one Tuesday afternoon.

I was sitting, exhausted and in pain, in our two-bedroom apartment when I heard a knock on the front door. Both Issy and Lulu were in the miserable throes of ear infections, and I had spent two hours scuttling between the pair of them, Issy in her own little room and Lulu in the alcove off our bedroom, desperately trying to tend to them both in the vain hope they would each nap. Both of the girls wanted to be on me, and it was physically impossible to appease them simultaneously. All three of us were catatonically sleep deprived. At the sound of the knock, I dared to dream that perhaps help was on its way. Perhaps someone – Nick, Mum, anyone – would be standing on my doorstep, swooping in to rescue me and the girls?

Lugging Lulu on my hip, I opened the door and discovered it was one of our neighbours from upstairs, and my heart sank as I registered the look on her face: a mixture of disgust and disdain.

'You and your husband seem like nice people but I cannot understand why you can't get your baby to stop crying, and it's not fair on us,' she said. 'What are you doing? You need to make her stop.'

I was mortified.

'I'm so sorry,' I said, choking back tears. 'The girls are both sick and I'm trying. I am trying so hard.'

'It's just not reasonable. I have study to do and I'm exhausted. I'm so sick of it.'

I understood. I really did. I was sick of it too. I wanted to cry and curl up in my bed for the day. She had articulated my absolute worst nightmare: that I was unfit to parent a baby and a toddler. That I was doing it wrong. I felt that. Desperately. And

I was shattered. Bone-tired in the way that's only possible when you haven't slept for longer than three hours in seven months. Her words gutted me.

The week before, given it had been such a hellish week with Lulu's sleep, we had left small parcels of rocky road and ear plugs at all of our neighbours' doors: a peace offering. We knew that apartment living brought challenges with it, and we knew that an unsettled baby was hardly the preferred backing track for any tenant. What we didn't have was anywhere else to go. Nor did we have a magical answer for how to make this little girl stop crying.

I closed the door and crumbled behind it. With Lulu on my lap, I sat with my back against the door and sobbed. Little Issy, my sweet companion, came out of her room and sat beside me.

'You 'kay, Mummy?' she asked with her big wide eyes, searing with love.

'Yeah, I'm okay. Mummy is just sad.'

She leant into me with her little body, and I cried. I wondered whether this invisible suburban mayhem was taking place in other homes around the country. How many other parents had felt this way?

It took genuine pluck to persevere that day, but out of necessity and love, like many parents in the trenches both before and after me, I did. It wasn't pretty and it wasn't easy, but I pushed through, going through the motions of the afternoon, pretending to be the patient mother I wished I could be. I was hopeful that easier times would soon come.

Even recounting that now, I feel a tug of resistance. I hear a voice inside my head reminding me that it is indulgent to complain about the privilege of caring for healthy children. In the book of life's hardships, raising little kids might not seem worthy of a mention, and yet the daily reality of persevering with little sleep, isolation and being overwhelmingly needed all the time can be far from idyllic. It can be stressful and lonely and testing and overwhelming. And it can be compounded by the expectation that you are supposed to be at your most content, cherishing every moment and milestone with your darling bundles.

Denying parents the physical and emotional tribulations that life with newborns and toddlers entails – even with the trappings of privilege – is cruel. For all the joy and love that it involves, it's bloody hard yakka too. I'm not unfamiliar with difficult times (read earlier chapters) but parenting a toddler and a baby is peculiarly demanding. Truthfully, the chapter of my life as an ostensibly solo parent with a toddler and a baby remains one of the more difficult times I have endured. I relied heavily on the lessons I extracted from rehab and had to consistently and intentionally lower the bar.

Perfectionism and parenting are not a natural mix, and I reminded myself of this often. On top of that, what is achievable with a toddler and a baby is vastly different from what is achievable in any other setting.

I tried to take my life day by day, hour by hour; to celebrate the small wins, any win, and to accept the losses. In some ways being in the domestic trenches with two under two lends itself to this way of life more than work does: when you are literally physically beholden to the constantly changing demands of little people, it forces an appreciation of the small things.

Having a moment alone in the bathroom feels momentous. A better-than-usual latte is life-affirming. A chat in the park with a fellow parent is joyful. Getting through a grocery shop without incident, a baby sleeping slightly longer than anticipated, having a moment to enjoy rather than cajole a toddler ... these are the little things that really make your day. And they are things that, in another setting, you might not even have noticed.

During this time, my blog remained a beloved sanity-saving hobby: it was cheaper than therapy, but still effective. Whenever the stars aligned and I had time to write something coherent, I published it. Having this little world in my head constructing posts was a happy distraction. By this stage, like at *BRW*, in addition to musing about life as a mum in the urban jungle, I had taken to writing rather often about broader issues for women. Feminism and sexism and the gendered expectations on men and women occupied a growing space in my mind and my work.

It was through this, and my unofficial capacity as *BRW*'s self-appointed advocate for women, that Marina Go had learned of my existence.

'If she wants to talk about a job on *Women's Agenda* I will actually die and go to heaven,' I told Nick as soon as he arrived back in Sydney on Sunday morning. 'You don't understand. Like, I will actually die!' Even the prospect of being considered for a job made me giddy. Two weeks after I had left *BRW* to go on maternity leave with Lulu, major personnel changes had been made at the magazine. Kate Mills was no longer the editor, and I wasn't exactly sure what those changes would have meant for me on my return, so I was open to something new, especially from a publication I so admired.

The next week, feverish with anticipation, I took off with Lulu to the meeting in Surry Hills. I had roped a friend in to walk Lulu around the block a few times in the pram so I could speak to Marina without having to think about settling her or needing to spill my breast from my shirt.

We sat in the dappled light of a cafe courtyard, its walls covered in climbing ivy, and ordered coffees.

'We are looking to appoint a maternity-leave cover to edit *Women's Agenda*, and I thought you would make a great fit,' she said after we'd dispensed with the small talk.

Me? Editing Women's Agenda?! To my mind it was the most perfect marriage of my blog writing and the more serious reporting I'd been doing for *BRW*. And the kicker was still to come.

'I know you have two small children and childcare can be an absolute nightmare, so you might have to tell us how it could work. But we'd love you to give it some thought,' Marina said. 'If you think you can do it, we'll make it work.'

There were more coffees, an interview with the founding editor, Angela Priestley, and some boxes to tick, but that moment was a game changer in my career. It was an opportunity offered at what many employers might deem the least opportune moment to stretch a female employee: while she is in the trenches of early parenting. But Marina knew, from her own experience working as an editor with her own young children, that the challenge was not insurmountable. An arrangement could be made that ensured the job would be done, and she suspected I'd be up to it. The role would start in late July, so I had time to line things up.

The timing was perfect. I was drowning at home under the weight of responsibility and the monotony of parenting a toddler and a baby, around the clock, not just Monday to Friday but weekends too. Living on a single income after my paid leave from *BRW* and the government ran out wasn't going to be sustainable either, so I was going to need to work again one way or another. And this was the job of my dreams.

I left that coffee meeting buzzing. *How does this even happen? How is it even possible to be offered a job so perfect? To be offered the flexibility and autonomy to design a work schedule around my family?*

Nick was overjoyed when I told him. Having witnessed the toll living in Oxford had taken on my professional confidence, and knowing the thrill I derived from writing and reporting, my job offer was a dream for him too. He knew as well as I did that I thrived with purpose and, he knew, better than I did, that I had potential to fulfil beyond being a mum.

Nick's professional ambition to become a surgeon was going to require huge sacrifices from us both. I was willing to support the hours of study over years that it would take for Nick to qualify as a surgeon, but I knew – particularly from our time overseas – that putting my own professional dreams on hold to do that wasn't a viable option. Even if we could have afforded to live on one wage, we both knew that our marriage and my mental health would be much better off with me engaged in work outside the home.

Nonetheless, I was nervous and began indulging in guilt about the job.

What sort of mother would get so excited about a job when she has a baby?

The fact someone articulated that very sentiment didn't help. Now and then I thought back to the corporate lawyer and stockbroker I'd nannied for all those years before, the four children they so rarely had the time to see – was that the kind of home we were creating?

Nick and my mum were ruthless in steering me away from that rabbit hole.

'If you don't take this role, honestly, you will regret it for years,' Nick said one night over dinner. 'I know you will.'

'Am I selfish, though? For wanting it?'

'Selfish for wanting to take an amazing job that you've been offered? No.'

'But selfish for not just wanting to stay home with the girls?'

'Am I selfish for wanting to be a surgeon?'

'You know I don't think that.'

It wasn't the first time Nick had asked me that question, nor was it the first time I said no. Wanting to be a surgeon requires a commitment and focus that is really difficult to reconcile with ordinary life. It necessitates selfishness in many ways, and having a family and a marriage on those terms isn't easy. I have resented his choice of vocation, deeply, on many occasions, but we've mostly been able to navigate the dynamic, for a few reasons: firstly, despite the disparity in contact hours, Nick has never treated my work or career as being less important than his. I would not have lasted thirty seconds in our marriage if that was the case. Secondly, Nick didn't choose surgery *because* of the gargantuan commitment it demands, he chose it because it's work he loves. For a man with every right to bemoan his working conditions, he never complains, because the work he does sets his world on fire. Finally, when Nick's time is his own, it's ours, without question.

Curiously, though, even with the horrendous hours Nick worked when my dream job was offered, I wasn't questioning *his* commitment to our kids. I only questioned myself.

What sort of mother would get so excited about this job? Me. This mother. A mum who knew intimately from her own lived experience that purpose matters. A woman who believes strenuously that financial independence isn't optional but critical. A mum who wants her kids to grow up accepting that careers are not gendered, that working and caring are shared pursuits of parents. A woman who is passionate about championing women to succeed and desperate to accelerate the glacial pace of change towards equality.

At this stage, six years after my *annus horribilis*, I wasn't just familiar with these various realities of my personality and psyche – I was accepting of them. And more than just wanting to be engaged in work, this job, editing *Women's Agenda*, satisfied another of my more radical desires.

Despite wanting, at times, for this not to be the case, I had come to discover that I actually had a little troublemaker inside me. It seemed that staying quiet and saying nothing wasn't actually my natural preference: the more I had written for *BRW* and my blog, the braver and more determined I had grown in my willingness to speak up. To ruffle feathers and challenge the status quo. I wrote a blistering opinion piece for *BRW* that the *Financial Review* also published on the hypocrisy of law firms paying lip service to supporting women while still punishing the victims of sexual harassment rather than holding the more powerful perpetrators to account. This was almost a full decade before #MeToo took off, and the subject matter was rarely in the papers. Many of the law firms I dealt with regularly were deeply unimpressed, but I was pleased to realise that I was genuinely unfazed by this.

After I wrote a cover story on the rare phenomenon that is the female CEO, and the barriers they face, I was approached by more than one male reporter at the company who wanted to explain to me why I was wrong. That women and men were given equal opportunities and the disparity in numbers was a reflection of women's choices.

In each case I took on the fight: no person, man or woman,

makes 'choices' in a vacuum, and the structural disadvantages women face in workplaces cannot be ignored. Nor can the cultural expectations of women.

When I wrote a report about the broken childcare system in Australia, I received a public rebuke from a Labor minister, but I took on the fight. It wasn't personal: the cost and unavailability of appropriate childcare positions was an issue that could and would deter women from working.

As far as I was concerned, things needed to change for women in Australia and an opportunity to work in a role where that was part of the remit was too good to pass up. The fact it didn't even feel especially brave is testament to how far I had evolved since I was too scared to resign from a job I hated because the tug of conformity was so strong.

I signed the contract and shortly afterwards began the most fantastic job I could ever have imagined. I realise that's the third time I have made that observation, but it's true!

I worked three shortish days in the office and a fourth day across the other two days, but even still, childcare was a nightmare to arrange.

Despite Lulu having been on a waiting list since she was fourteen weeks in utero, there was no position for her at the centre Issy attended, and a position was unlikely to be available until the following year.

I rang two-dozen childcare centres near our apartment and my prospective office, and just as many family day care places (where the care takes place in a home environment, rather than a centre), all to no avail.

Getting a nanny looked to be the only viable option, until I did the maths. Engaging a nanny for ten hours a day – which, by the time I factored in the physical handovers and the commute to and from work, allowed for eight hours in the office – cost upwards of $250 after tax with no rebate available. Outlaying $750 a week for three days of childcare might have been affordable for some families, but not for many and certainly not for ours.

Just before I was due to start, one of our neighbours, an accountant who was also struggling to find care to facilitate her return to work, mentioned that she had recently been offered two days with a nearby family day care home for her ten-month-old daughter. She had turned it down because the only two days available were the days she already had care secured. I rang immediately and felt lucky when they offered me two days a week, which, combined with Issy's three days at the childcare centre and a nanny one day a week, would give me coverage to do my job.

It lasted two weeks before the logistical madness of doing two separate drop-offs rendered the arrangement ridiculous. Illness struck Lulu on her second day in care, which then meant she was unable to attend for another whole week. A steady comedy of errors and a roundabout of illnesses meant arriving at work in those early weeks in the job felt nothing short of miraculous.

What might have worked on paper wasn't working in reality. Having the girls cared for in two distant suburbs was not sustainable. The simple act of getting two children under three in and out of the car four times in a day was in itself a challenge, but throw in illness, traffic, the joy of finding parks outside the relevant centres, doing the actual drop-offs, and then making my way to the office – in another suburb again – was ludicrous.

Despite the fact it was not – in the short term – affordable, employing a nanny to mind Lulu was the only option. (A nanny also became slightly more affordable when we calculated what we had spent on the days we ended up paying for two separate day care centres *and* a nanny because the girls were not well enough to attend the centres.) We ended up striking the nannying lottery and engaged a delightful Brazilian woman who had recently married an Australian man.

She was gentle and patient with the girls, who both adored her, she was willing and able to wrest with our 'spirited' baby, and she cooked and folded washing to boot. Her arrival meant getting out the door in the morning became an exercise in joy, and I no longer found myself wanting to cry or quietly rock back and forth before 8am. Similarly, arriving home in the late afternoon on those days became something I looked forward to. I didn't need to cart a work handbag, two backpacks, a fractious baby and a thundering toddler through the door, ready to embark on the 'second shift'. I could simply knock at the door and wait to be greeted by two happy little girls ready to be fed and played with before bed.

I am – still – acutely aware of my privilege here. Having a nanny toiling away on the home front while you're at work *is* a luxury. But working outside the home without any help *inside* the home while raising little kids in a big city – without family nearby or the scaffolding of community to step in and share the load – *is* ludicrous. From a purely mathematical perspective, hiring a nanny didn't make sense. It ate into a good chunk of our earnings, but it was an investment that facilitated my return to work.

We didn't need a nanny forever because once a place became available for Lulu at the same centre Issy attended, they both went there, and our childcare bill dropped. In practical terms, by the time that came around Lulu was four months older, sleeping more and was slightly more placable.

The irony of almost not being able to take a job with an organisation championing the success of women in the workplace purely because I couldn't access childcare was not lost on me. It strengthened my resolve to advocate for change for women – even if that wasn't going to make me particularly popular. The fact that as I started my job, an election campaign kicked off that saw Australia elect Tony Abbott as prime minister, meant there was more reason than ever to actively speak up and speak out for the rights of women.

In my role at *Women's Agenda*, aside from writing and publishing political commentary and news, I also had cause to contemplate material relating to career success. We engaged a number of leading coaches to run webinars for our readers and write advice for women looking for success at work. Two subjects that came up regularly were the power of connecting with purpose, and strengths-based leadership. To put it crudely, both revolved around the notion that when an individual feels authentically connected to their work, and when they are working in a way that suits their natural strengths, they are far more likely to succeed. It makes sense: working with the grain – as opposed to against it – is energising rather than energy-depleting.

To me, this provides an academic answer for something that happened after I fell apart. As a lawyer I felt like a square peg desperately trying to squeeze into a round hole, which isn't a battle that working in journalism has ever presented. To the contrary, from the minute I arrived in journalism, it felt natural: it felt like I was doing what I was supposed to be doing.

Perhaps it's merely a coincidence that this happened, but it seems to me that an unexpected upside to downsizing the toxic baggage I had lugged around for too many years was that it freed me up to enjoy life – and even succeed – in ways I hadn't thought possible. By being clear about what I really wanted, I was able to thrive.

Back to breaking point

July 2017

'I think I need help. I need to see someone.'

The light was out and Nick was almost asleep, so I whispered it, in the hope he might not hear me. He did.

'That sounds like a very good idea,' he said, rolling over to face me.

'I can't do this anymore.'

'I know. It's too much.' He stroked my hair as I cried. 'Let's call the GP tomorrow and make an appointment for early next week when we're back. She'll be able to recommend someone good, and you can get a health care plan.'

I'd been thinking about this for weeks but hadn't been able to bring myself to say it out loud, in part because I knew that once I made the admission, I couldn't take it back. It would make me accountable.

We were in Yamba for a week over the winter school holidays, but it was far from idyllic. Though my Crohn's disease had been lying entirely dormant for ten years, after my fall when Lulu was a baby, I had developed rheumatoid arthritis in my right sacroiliac joint, where the hip and spine meet, which I discovered was a new manifestation of the disease. It is estimated that around 20 per cent of Crohn's patients will develop arthritis in a major joint, and I found myself in that select group. The fact my digestion remained perfectly ordinary cushioned the blow somewhat.

After much trial and error, and nearly eighteen months in chronic and debilitating pain, I was eventually put on a course of medication that managed the condition so well that I could exercise and function normally again without an iota of pain. After half a year of this, in the middle of 2015, it seemed possible to try for the third baby we had always hoped for.

By this time, we had moved and were renting a bigger place across the bridge, which meant we had space. We didn't have neighbours living on top of us or sharing a wall with us, and not having to worry about imposing the cacophony of family life on anyone else was wonderful.

We knew a third pregnancy might make the pain flare up, which it did, but we assumed that after I'd had the baby it would settle down again. After an easy pregnancy, an easy labour, and the easiest baby we'd ever taken delivery of – another delicious daughter, Ruby – the pain was something I figured would eventually subside. It didn't.

I spent the first year of Ruby's life on steroids, which kept the pain at bay but wasn't a sustainable solution because of the adverse side effects. When she turned one and I stopped breastfeeding, I stopped taking steroids and started trialling an alternative. The pain returned immediately, but initially I was able to cope because of my mistaken assumption that it would be temporary. I'd been told my new wonder drug had a twelve-week 'waiting period' before I would feel any relief, so I waited it out.

Fast forward four months without any relief, and I was in a bad way. My ability to cope was being stretched.

Running a household, working and taking care of three children under six is plenty on its own, but with pain it's ridiculous. But the existence of small children for whom I was responsible also meant there was no escape route: I couldn't exactly flee to Mum and Dad's for a few months this time. I had no choice but to wake up each day and push ahead as best I could.

On holidays, without the distraction of our ordinary routine, I fell in a heap. I didn't have to persevere like I did at home, because Nick was around. I didn't have to push on and ignore the pain because there weren't school drop-offs to juggle, or deadlines to meet, or meals to prepare. These realities had kept me from confronting what became impossible to ignore once we were on holiday: I wasn't coping. The pain was debilitating, my patience had run out and I was bitterly disappointed that none of the treatments was helping. I was in a bad place, and while it wasn't a 'gotta go back to rehab' bad place, I knew it wasn't far from it.

When we were back home, I made an appointment with my GP. Thanks to my having three small children who required immunisations, weigh-ins and check-ups at regular intervals, we'd managed to foster a friendship. She was warm, professional and totally approachable, but as I sat in the waiting room, anticipating my name being called, a sense of foreboding came over me.

I didn't want to tell this woman that I wasn't coping. I didn't want to say the words. I didn't want to have to talk about my mental state. I had grown accustomed to playing the role of engaged and responsible parent at this medical practice and switching to the role of a mother who wasn't coping filled me with dread.

When she called me in, we exchanged the usual pleasantries before we both sat down. Then the pause arrived. My heart thumped and I blinked back tears as I made out the words I had been desperate to avoid saying.

'I'm not coping. I've found the past few months really, really difficult, and the truth is I'm struggling.'

I cried as I said that I thought I needed to see someone to help me manage. She could not have been more understanding.

'Georgie, I am honestly surprised it's taken you this long to hit this wall. Chronic pain is enough to tip anyone into distress.'

I nodded as she passed me the box of tissues.

'The fact you have managed as long as you have is quite remarkable, but I think seeking help is a great idea.'

I left that day with a referral to see Amanda, a psychologist who specialised in treating people with physical illness, but also with a reminder that fragile mental health is *so* hard to talk about. Even when you are a person who has openly talked about the fact mental health has been an issue for you, like I have, it can be paralysing. There remains a stigma attached to mental illness that is readily understood when you have personally been affected by it. Immense personal shame attaches itself to the feelings that anxiety and depression trigger, and there is a sense that these feelings amount to a failure of sorts. That if you were stronger or better you wouldn't suffer this way. This shame and failure just compound the pain.

Talking about this, admitting that you think you have a problem, is a hurdle that can feel entirely insurmountable when you are in the grips of an episode. For a person in the throes of depression, doing *anything* is difficult. All those years before, when I had sunk into a deep depression before I finally went to rehab, just thinking about having a shower was an effort. It took everything I had to make that happen, and once it was done, I was completely exhausted. Given that tiny, everyday, non-threatening tasks like showering and brushing your hair become massive achievements for a person experiencing depression, can you even begin to imagine how hard it is to get yourself to a doctor? And to then admit how you are feeling?

It is akin to standing on a stage in front of every person you have ever met and taking off your clothes, one item at a time. It is frightening, and the very definition of vulnerability. I know this because I have lived it. I also know that ignoring mental illness isn't a preferable alternative. Seeking help, no matter how uncomfortable it feels, no matter how much courage it requires, *is* the way to feel better.

Aside from the shame and vulnerability that delayed me seeking psychological support when I needed it, there was another factor behind my reluctance to get help this time around. Despite having experienced – first-hand – the remarkable and practical rewards of seeing a good psychologist, when it came to this predicament – managing chronic pain – I didn't believe therapy would be of any use. I was sure that until the pain itself was resolved – fixed or at least minimised – I was destined to occupy a compromised psychological state.

If that strikes you as being similar to the line I doggedly pursued regarding my vertigo – that until the dizziness was fixed, my mental health didn't matter – that's because it is. It's practically identical, and because I am a fallible human being I returned to this perilous ground *again*. I very seriously doubted there was anything a psychologist could do or say that would help me in the increasingly hostile battle that daily life had become.

The very first appointment with Amanda proved my misgivings wrong and reminded me that 'talking' really is so much more than just saying words. Obviously, the articulate and compassionate woman opposite me couldn't wave a wand and make the pain go away, but she *could* help me unpack what that pain was doing, and that in itself was constructive. Between my head, my heart and my hip was a blur of angst and anger and sadness.

She offered the invaluable ear of a totally objective stranger to whom I could open up without fear of burdening someone I loved. My battle with pain – which sadly persists – was lonely. In the confines of my mind, being in pain was a weakness, a cruel burden on my kids, on Nick, my parents and siblings. Proof, once more, that I was faulty goods. Putting words around the anger and the fear that stemmed from all of that was terrifying, but also cathartic.

Amanda made me see that my struggle was valid. I was still expecting the same things from myself that I would have expected if I was well. I felt tremendously guilty that I couldn't walk Issy to school like I always had, that I couldn't play actively, that taking the kids to the park and battling the pram and swings and lifting and twisting were all completely beyond my limits. I hated how I craved the end of each day, not because the pain would disappear, but because I could at least stop moving.

These limitations on my body felt like terrible indictments on my capacity as a mother and a wife. It wasn't especially logical, but it was compelling – at least until this woman explained that I was basically starting every day on empty and pushing ahead regardless.

I wasn't sleeping well because of the discomfort of my inflamed joint, which started the day fairly irked and then became increasingly angry hour by hour, until it reached a nasty crescendo of incandescent rage by 5pm, at which point I would be desperate to collapse, all the while resenting myself for not being able to cope better. Amanda said the fact there was any parenting, work, cooking, socialising or laundering happening in the middle of this was something of a miracle, and because she was in effect an objective bystander, I believed her.

She made me realise that I was grieving: I was mourning for the me who could bounce out of bed without even thinking about a joint in my hip that I once – blissfully – had no idea existed. I was, once more, in the thick of chronic illness, and while that was far from a happy realisation, it was a necessary one.

I had fixated on the idea that our kids shouldn't have a mum compromised by illness – nor Nick a wife – and yet I had bypassed the salient fact that, on that line of thinking, I shouldn't have had to put up with illness either.

So too, the fact that what might be ideal doesn't always correlate with reality. I needed to be told that having a mum with diminished physical capacity wasn't an abominable fate for children, as long as they remained loved and cared for. I needed to be reminded that life is not perfect, and that that was as true for my kids as it was for Nick and me.

A mum in chronic pain certainly isn't the worst fate a child can face, but it does require compromise, whether they consciously compute it that way or not. I needed to be told that as well as the many negative conclusions I had drawn about our kids missing out, my health was also planting seeds in them for empathy and resilience.

It is ludicrous, but paying to sit on Amanda's couch and cry my heart out was some of the best money I've ever spent. I walked away from every appointment with tear-stained cheeks and puffy eyes, still in pain and still in fear, but lighter. With perspective. With the understanding that I was facing something difficult, which didn't fix the pain, but at least helped me to handle it.

Around the time I was seeing Amanda, I signed the contract to write this book, and despite the fact it was professionally and personally very exciting, I deliberately didn't mention it to her. And nor did I mention my health struggles to the publisher.

I struggled with straddling two different worlds: my personal world, in which illness was wreaking havoc and rendering me helpless and hopeless, and my work world, in which life carried on. The dichotomy – of being sick but still capable – felt fraudulent, because in my head one ought to have cancelled the other out. How could I possibly be in the midst of an exciting work project while I was simultaneously in the midst of debilitating pain?

The reality of chronic illness is, of course, more nuanced. For me, it is possible to be succeeding and failing at once. There are times when it isn't possible for me to straddle both worlds – where my condition, or the treatments required for it, necessitate retreating from work and parenting and persevering. Sometimes I need to pull the doona up and succumb. When that happens, the trick is to remember that it's not forever. That it's a moveable feast. That life doesn't stay still.

Anxiety was – and remains – a far bigger issue for me than depression, but the black dog does still visit from time to time, and pain is something of a magnet for it.

Medically, depression is defined as 'a mood disorder that causes a persistent feeling of sadness and loss of interest'. It can be called a major depressive disorder or clinical depression, and it affects how a person feels, thinks and behaves, and can lead to a variety of emotional and physical problems. A person suffering from depression may have trouble doing normal day-to-day activities and feel like life isn't worth living.

It isn't a weakness, nor is it a state a person can just 'snap out of', as they are occasionally told to by well-meaning friends and family members. It has to be experienced to be properly understood: in my experience, it is pervasive, scary and horribly sticky. It feels hard to move. Hard to breathe. Hard to think. It often isn't until the fog lifts that I am able to recognise how deflated I have been feeling: how difficult life is under the heavy blanket of depression.

Generally, depression results from a combination of recent events and other long-term or personal factors, rather than one immediate issue or event. Continuing difficulties like long-term unemployment, living in an abusive or uncaring relationship, isolation or loneliness, or prolonged work stress are more likely to cause depression than recent life stresses. But a recent event – like losing your job – or a combination of events can 'trigger' depression if you're already at risk.

Although there's been a lot of research in the field, much remains unknown about depression. It isn't as simple as a 'chemical imbalance'. Factors including genetic vulnerability, severe life stressors, substances you may take (some medications, drugs and alcohol) and medical conditions can affect the way a brain regulates a person's moods. Most modern anti-depressants have an effect on your brain's chemical transmitters (serotonin and noradrenaline), which relay messages between brain cells – this is thought to be how medications work for more severe depression. Psychological treatment can also help you to regulate your moods. Effective treatment can stimulate the growth of new nerve cells in circuits that regulate your mood, which is thought to play a critical part in recovering from the most severe episodes of depression.

The good news is treatment is known to be effective, not at curing mental illness but in making it easier to grapple with – which my lived experience reflects. While there is no sure way to prevent depression, there are several strategies that can help. Controlling stress, reaching out to family and friends, and seeking help early are all useful.

Being aware of what constitutes mental illness is also useful. Not every one of life's challenging periods will result in anxiety or depression, in the same way that anxiety and depression don't need to be triggered by anything specific. It is possible to go through life and endure all manner of tragedies and challenges without ever suffering a moment's trouble with your mental health. Similarly, it is possible to live a life free from tragedy and still be plagued by depression and anxiety. If you are in the former category, count your blessings. If that's not you and you have been, or you are, affected, the good news is that mental illness is treatable. Not necessarily quickly or easily, but it is possible to manage.

But because you fixed something once doesn't mean it won't ever crop up again. Annoyingly, breaking once didn't provide a guarantee that I wouldn't break again. Getting treatment for anxiety and depression once, sadly, wasn't a 'set and forget' exercise. It was something I have had to return to, and I will in all likelihood return to many times again.

It is hard to imagine a person would ever snap their leg in two and avoid medical treatment. The same goes for a great big laceration on the arm, a shocking flu or a raging ear infection. These ailments, in the main, would swiftly send most people in the direction of medical assistance. But the same still cannot be said of individuals suffering from depression and anxiety. Despite there being some disbelief about that, if you've ever experienced either or both of these conditions, this is not difficult to understand. Not even close.

Metamorphosis

September 2013

> *I'd rather get aids than watch your cousin.*

> *Who is the dumb bitch?*

> *Why is this ugly feminazi even allowed on TV?*

> *I feel sorry for her husband. He's probably gay and that's why she hates men.*

It was just after 10pm on a Sunday night and I had just stepped off the set at Sky News, oblivious to the storm I'd just been caught in. As the acting editor of *Women's Agenda* I had been invited to be part of a panel to discuss the weekend's stories. That day, I had anxiously waited to receive the topics we'd be discussing during the hour-long live-to-air program. I read all the weekend papers back to front, I scoured the web, and then, when the topics came through, I knuckled down and read the twelve or so stories that were listed.

The issues we'd be discussing ranged from Tony Abbott's sleeping quarters in Canberra, to an essay former Prime Minister Julia Gillard had written for *The Guardian*, to Syria, to gun control, to the Labor leadership, to lowering the legal age for teenagers to serve alcohol. It was a mixed bag, so I read and thought and read and thought some more. That Sunday, while wrangling the girls and going about our day, I thought at length about the issues we'd likely be discussing. I wanted to be prepared.

My biggest fear was being asked a question and not having a reasonable answer. I knew my views would not be the consensus among the panellists, so I was particularly keen to have reasonable responses at the ready. I didn't necessarily set out to change anyone's mind, but I wanted to be informed, measured and rational. Aside from not wanting to humiliate myself on television, I wanted to make it difficult for my point of view to be dismissed out of hand.

It turns out I had worried about the wrong things. The conversation was heated, as I had expected, but I thought I had kept my cool and held my own. I was almost always in disagreement with the three men I sat with, but neither the host, Paul, nor my two fellow panellists were nasty, and they were very friendly as we left the set and I bid them goodbye. As I walked away, Paul called out, 'Ignore anything ugly on Twitter!'

I knew my boss, Marina, had been watching, along with Mum, Dad and Nick, and I was eager to get their read on how it went. But as I reached into my handbag, I noticed my phone was off, which struck me as strange: it had been fully charged an hour earlier when I had turned it onto silent.

Once I was in the car I plugged it in and waited for it to come back to life. The text messages that popped up alerted me to a problem.

> Well done G. Ignore the haters. Love Dad.

> Are you ok darling? Twitter is AWFUL!!! Who are these people??? Nick

> Georgie, well done. You were calm and compelling. I have been fighting the trolls all night. xx Marina.

> G, We couldn't watch because we don't have Sky but the comments on Facebook are appalling. I hope you're ok. Meg

It turned out that my phone had melted down thanks to trolls in the Twittersphere taking issue with everything from my ideas to my earrings to my appearance, to my very existence.

Before I could digest too many of the revolting sentiments popping up on my phone I called Nick via Bluetooth so we could chat as I made my way home.

'Are you okay? I've been trying to ring,' he said.

'Yeah. My phone turned itself off so I haven't seen everything, but it looks like it got quite nasty on Twitter?'

'You were really good! As soon as the show started the tweets came through on that column and it didn't stop. Who are these people?'

'I'm not sure.'

'Stop and buy ice-cream. You deserve it and I need it.'

Hours earlier, before I had left home to make my way to the Sky studio in Macquarie, Nick had asked me to set my laptop up so he could watch Twitter as well as the show itself. At the time I had no inkling it would add a wholly unpleasant dimension to the evening. All I had hoped was that I wouldn't make an idiot of myself. He'd never had any involvement with the platform, and given the avalanche of abuse that followed, it was hardly a heartwarming first taste.

My workmates from *Women's Agenda,* my extended family and close friends were all quick to send texts or emails with kind messages of support. I felt grateful not to be arriving home to an empty flat. Nick was waiting with spoons at the ready to demolish the medicinal Ben & Jerry's I had brought home.

He was flabbergasted that anyone would take the time to hate a stranger on their television screen with such gusto. 'Why don't they just change the channel?'

I shrugged. 'Because they love to hate.'

The hatred was astonishing to behold. I didn't read every single message, but there were hundreds laced with spite and vitriol and contempt.

I was a bitch. A ditz. Ugly. Stupid. Dumb.

Later that night I lay awake, unable to sleep, with all of those vicious words swirling through my mind. It was rattling and deeply unpleasant but, strangely, I didn't feel shame. I felt shocked. I knew I did not get trolled because I had made a fool of myself. Yes I was a novice at being on TV, but I didn't mess up or invent things: I was articulate and measured.

The trouble was, largely, that I had expressed support for former Prime Minister Julia Gillard, who had written a piece about Labor's troubles following their defeat in the 2013 election: a lightning rod for woman-hating trolls. Personally, I felt my point was nuanced: had Gillard merely wanted to throw petrol on the flames of the fire engulfing her party, she could have used every opportunity throughout the federal election to do so. She could have held doorstops, released statements and used social media to punish her former colleagues. (A route other former prime ministers have happily taken.) But Gillard didn't do that. She stayed silent throughout the election, and a month on from the result she published a 5000-word think piece thoughtfully examining where things had gone wrong for Labor, including an acknowledgement of the role she had played in that.

A woman expressing that opinion was unwelcome. On this particular evening, the trolls, who were all men, hated the message that Gillard's voice might be credible and that she had every right to exercise it, and they hated the messenger more.

The most unsettling part was that while they might have been anonymous and had very few followers, they were not robots. They might have been hiding behind computer screens or mobile phones to fling their insults, but they were still real people. And some of them clearly harboured a deep hatred of women, which was both terrifying and fortifying to consider. At least the abuse I faced wasn't about me; it was about the views and values I stood for.

This ugly torrent of hate and disdain for women was not

something I was willing to countenance, so when I was invited back on the show the next week I said yes – and the next time and the next time. If I was being offered a platform to discuss issues from a perspective I felt was too often dismissed or downplayed, I was going to take it. The trolling was never again as merciless as it was on that first night, but it was persistent. Occasionally, whether it's triggered by a TV appearance, a column I've written or a tweet I've posted, the trolling can still be brutal. I'm not immune to feeling rattled by it, either: there have been times when seeing awful things written about me has led me to tears, to doubt, to discomfort. I doubt any feeling human could avoid that. And while I have withdrawn at times, and put up boundaries to protect myself, I haven't let it silence me.

Over time I did more TV. The ABC invited me on *The Drum*, *Weekend Breakfast* and even *Lateline* on Budget Night to talk about the economic impact of the new policies on women. *The Today Show* and *Weekend Sunrise* invited me on at different points too. Being a talking head in the media happened gradually, unfolding organically as a result of the field I worked in, and it's only when I step back and consider where I was ten years ago that I realise how much I have changed.

Ten years ago, I would not have survived the mortification of being publicly dissected over social media. It wouldn't have ever happened, for starters, because I would never have accepted an invitation to appear on TV. The risk of public humiliation would have been too high to even consider. Now, I can't fathom *not* speaking out about the things I believe in.

~

'Mummy, was today one of your book days?' Lulu, aged six, asked, perched on one of the stools at the kitchen bench, waiting for dinner.

'Yep,' I answered, while serving up spaghetti bolognese into the three bowls I had out for each of the girls.

'How many words did you write today?' Issy asked.

'I hit my target.' I smiled, knowing the reaction this would spark.

'One thousand, five hundred?'

'Yep!'

'Good job!' Issy beamed back at me.

This exchange was a nightly ritual. Ruby was too young to participate in the questions, but Issy and Lulu alternately quizzed me on what my work day entailed:

Did I work in the city?

Write for Women's Agenda?

Do a podcast?

Go on TV?

Do my newspaper column?

Their curiosity and enthusiasm were infectious, and fielding their questions was a genuine perk of parenting.

'What's your book about again, Mum?' Lulu asked. 'Is it about us?'

'Well, it's not about you, but each of you is in it,' I replied.

'It's about a time Mummy got sick,' Issy said. 'Was it a heart attack?'

I couldn't help but laugh. My amazingly fit and healthy Dad had shocked us all two years earlier when he had a heart attack in a spin class, embedding the term in Issy's vernacular. He'd needed open-heart surgery, which was a terrifying ordeal – particularly for Mum, ever the dutiful carer. Fortunately Dad, who is Gaga to his grandkids, emerged intact and made a full recovery. With his errant valves repaired, he actually started to feel far better than he had in years.

'No, darling. Gaga had a heart attack, I had a nervous breakdown.'

'Oh. Which is worse?' Issy enquired.

I laughed again.

'That's a good question,' I said. 'I didn't need to have a big operation like Gaga, but I did have to go to a hospital. They are different types of sickness but neither is very fun. My book is about how I got sick and how I got better.'

'So is it going to be called *How to be healthy?*' Lulu asked, matter-of-fact, between mouthfuls of pasta. 'It should be. That's a good name.'

It's not the title we landed on, but it's not too far off the mark.

My life can be divided neatly into two distinct phases: before breakdown, and after breakdown. Unhealthy and healthy. There were plenty of things that stayed the same, but the manner in which I approached my life was fundamentally different. In an ideal world I wouldn't have had to become so unwell in order to effect change, but I know that without that low, I probably wouldn't have shifted direction as radically as I did.

Hitting rock bottom, and staying there for several long and miserable months, changed my paradigm completely. It was a circuit-breaker that shocked me into confronting the uncomfortable truth that I had trashed my mental health to the point where it compromised my physical wellbeing.

As a result, I approached my recovery zealously. I was like a dog with a bone and, finally, it seemed I tapped into a constructive and positive outlet for my determination. I set about building my resilience and self-worth block by block, and recovery was the ultimate prize. Years later, I discovered that my experiences were backed by scientific evidence: it was possible to build resilience, and some of the techniques I had employed to achieve this were among the most effective.

When I speak about my breakdown, many people tell me that my story hits incredibly close to home for them. It mirrors what they see happening to young people in their lives: anxiety, pressure and perfectionism circling in a perfect storm. I try to tell these people that there is some good news. Often the characteristics that make a young person susceptible to burn-out or breakdown can be exactly what allows them to heal.

When I put my mind to it, I was able to make change happen. When I took some of the energy I had exerted on doing the right things, ticking the right boxes and living up to impossible standards, and shifted it to taking care of myself, I was able to create change. I took the medication I was prescribed, I took therapy seriously and I treated my psychological wellbeing and health as my priority.

Within a year of my stay in a psychiatric hospital, I was living a life that was better than I had ever imagined. I know how insufferable that sounds, but it was true. Even when I was working full-time again, with deadlines and the pressure of mastering a new vocation, I was able to hold stress at bay. Perhaps this was due in part to my new workplaces, which though hardly carefree, were far less hierarchical and formal than law firms. Even so, newsrooms aren't exactly known for being relaxed workplaces, and stress still became something that I felt from time to time, rather than something I could not escape.

The fact that ten years have passed since then without so much as a referral to a psychiatrist is proof that *something* in rehab worked for me. When I have experienced psychological distress in the past decade, it hasn't escalated into a full-blown catastrophe that's required intervention, and I don't think that's happened by chance. My health was a priceless vase that I had once dropped and watched shatter into a million pieces. Now, miraculously, it was repaired, and I wasn't going to risk dropping it ever again.

How I felt was a gauge that I regularly checked, and feeling good remained an objective. If I was feeling particularly anxious, I would tune in and try to figure out why that was the case. I would call upon my CBT toolkit and create a path out, or I would go for a walk or a swim. If my stomach was upset, I would revert to the foods that I knew helped. If I was irritable or panicked, I would breathe.

Ten years later, I can't pretend that I wake up with the same intense level of perspective and energy as I did when I first left rehab. When it comes to exercise, my arthritis has made it difficult to work out, which is one of the biggest burdens of the chronic pain to which I have become accustomed. But even before it set in, my efforts weren't quite as supercharged as they had been in the earliest post-rehab days. It took close to twelve months after my breakdown for me to resume a more regular existence, where my gratitude for merely being able to function waned. I did slip back into a life more ordinary, but not a life in which my health went unconsidered.

This all sounds incredibly patronising, I know. Eat your greens. Prioritise sleep. Move your body. Manage stress. It's the nauseating stuff we have all seen and read a million times before. It's the stuff I used to scoff at as utterly discretionary, but when I was forced into living those words, rather than denigrating them from the sidelines, my existence improved significantly. A person shouldn't need to break down to benefit from the lessons I learned the hard way – lessons that come naturally to some lucky folk. I married a person like that, and almost daily I am reminded that our wiring is different. I need to actively work to protect my mental health, and while that could be a source of angst in itself, it is a fact of life that is easier to accept than avoid. I am who I am, and sometimes I need to be told to eat my greens.

That in itself is a realisation that is both mortifyingly simple and incredibly powerful, and took me a long battle to reach. So too, discovering that the very best thing I could do for myself was to be my own friend. It shouldn't have been life-changing to realise this, but cast your eye over the self-help section at any library and you'll see that the simplest of life's lessons really are the hardest to grasp.

We are all fallible and we all have limits, and unfortunately we cannot remove ourselves entirely from harm's way. There is no single hard-and-fast rule that will protect a person in times of trouble, but there are ways we can give ourselves a little insulation and infrastructure. When the wind blows, which it will, how you recover will depend on whether you have a house of straw or a house of bricks. Back then, as a struggling 24-year-old, my mind was a house of straw that collapsed under pressure. I didn't realise it at the time, but in the weeks and months that followed I was forced to build a new house. Brick by brick, I put myself back together.

Acknowledgements

What a sweet relief it is to reach this page. Until I embarked on the actual process of writing a book, I hadn't grasped what it would entail. I'd heard it compared to having a child, but this has been unlike any of my pregnancies and looks nothing like my daughters.

Book-writing is an exceptionally solitary endeavour but ultimately, eventually, it takes a village.

My first thank you is significant and goes to Aviva Tuffield, the wonderful woman who approached me several years ago asking if I'd like to write a book. Just being asked was an honour, particularly when the question came from Aviva. When we first discussed it I was heavily pregnant and decided, wisely in hindsight, that the only project I really wanted to pursue during my third, and final, stint of parental leave was my baby. That decision, to simply focus on my family, was a delight to live out. When Ruby was approaching her first birthday and I was openly exploring the world of work again, Aviva got back in touch. *Breaking Badly* was born during a brief coffee in the middle of the Sydney Writer's Festival and would never have happened if it wasn't for Aviva's support and encouragement. Thank you.

The manuscript was less than halfway done when I met Martin Hughes from Affirm Press who happily took it – and its fledgeling author – under his wing. From the minute we first spoke on the phone I was struck by his warmth and enthusiasm which was, and has remained, incredibly encouraging.

To my editor Ruby Ashby-Orr, you are a wizard. Thank you for understanding me, for deciphering what I was trying to say and guiding me closer to what I needed to say on every page. It is humbling to consider the colossal difference between my first draft and this final version, thanks to your handiwork.

To Mum and Dad. Literally no day has passed where I haven't felt grateful to have you both in my corner, and never more so than when I fell part on your couch and didn't leave. I don't know what I would have done without you. Your love, kindness and support, not just of me, but of all of us and everyone you've ever met, is legendary. I love you both so much. Thank you for not only supporting me through hell, but for also supporting me when I forced you to relive that precise version of hell by writing a book about it.

To Belinda and Chris and Kris, it's unoriginal but you are the very best siblings a girl could ask for. You have always managed to offer me exactly what I've needed when I needed it most. Whether it's been a hug, a parcel of rocky road, moxibustion sticks, a midnight phonecall or something to laugh about, you have never failed to deliver. I love you all so much.

To my extended family and family friends who not only enthusiastically pitched in to help when I fell apart, but who also supported Mum and Dad in a million different ways, thank you. Pa. Sally. Meg. Miggy. All the Lismore BFFs. Together you form the most extraordinary safety net any person could hope to fall back on.

Writing this book gave me cause to reflect on the various friends that played different roles before, during and after my low point. It reminded me how spoiled I have been, all my life, in the incredible company I have been lucky enough to keep. Cass, Harry, Cath A, Rach, Vanessa, Courtney, Mandy, Libby, Hodge, Cath M, Sal H, Sam, Michelle, Amber, Annie, Alfonso, Cynthia, Cathy, Sal, Evie, Ruth, Sarah, Claire, Juliet, Tarla, Ange, Erin: each of you has coloured my world in different ways at different times, and I'm so grateful for the friendship we share. If I could shrink the world every now and again to bring you all physically closer, I would. Often.

To the people who have either championed my career or made my working days that much more enjoyable, thank you. Sean Aylmer, Kate Mills, Marina Go, Angela Priestley, Carol Schwartz, Mia Freedman, Kate de Brito, Holly Wainwright, Tracey Spicer, Lucy Ormonde, Caitlin Fitzsimmons, Lana Hirschowitz, Jenna Price, Helen Conway, Wendy McCarthy, Jess Gardner, Sam Hutchinson, JV Douglas, Kirstin Ferguson, Jane Caro, Catherine Fox.

To Annabel Crabb. The Annabel Crabb. A woman for whom no single label suffices: an indefatigable, kind, sharp, funny, generous, all-singing, all-dancing package of a human being. I will never fathom how, in between everything you do, not only did you find time to read this, but you liked it enough to put your name on it. There is not a name I could be prouder to have on the cover. Thank you seems woefully inadequate to convey my gratitude.

To Issy, my delightfully cheerful human word counter, Lulu, my hysterical and lovable firecracker, and Ruby, my deliciously affectionate big 'tid. Thank you for being the most curious, unique, funny and enthusiastic cheerleaders a mother could hope for. Each of you makes my heart sore and soar in ways I didn't imagine was possible.

I can't tell you how much I hope you never need to rely on the lessons I learned the hard way, but if you do – and you might – rest assured I'll try my very best to be the patient and steadfast carer you need. (I got a masterclass from your dad and Janny and Gaga, so you'll be fine.)

Finally, Nick. I'm sorry you didn't get to choose a pseudonym for the book. (Even if the publishers had allowed it, you were never going to be Rex.) Thank you for having the most enormous heart in the world. Thank you for supporting me every day back then as much as you have every day since. The support and encouragement and love you give me and our girls daily has to be experienced to be believed. That support is, like you, a force of nature, and it has made everything possible. I love you more than you could possibly know.

www.ingramcontent.com/pod-product-compliance
Lightning Source LLC
Chambersburg PA
CBHW021145160426
43194CB00007B/692